NICHOLAS WRIGHT

Nicholas Wright trained as an actor, and joined the Royal
Court Theatre in London as Casting Director before becoming
the first Director of the Court's Theatre Upstairs, where he
presented an influential programme of new and first-time
writing.

From 1975 to 1977 he was joint Artistic Director of the Royal
Court. He joined the National Theatre in 1984 as Literary
Manager and was an Associate Director of the National until
1998.

His plays include *Treetops* and *One Fine Day* (Riverside
Studios), *The Gorky Brigade* (Royal Court), *The Crimes of
Vautrin* (Joint Stock), *The Custom of the Country* and *The
Desert Air* (both Royal Shakespeare Company), *Cressida*
(Almeida Theatre at the Albery), *Mrs Klein* and *Vincent in
Brixton* (National Theatre and West End).

His versions of Ibsen's *John Gabriel Borkman* and Chekhov's
Three Sisters were seen at the National Theatre, and his
versions of Pirandello's *Naked* and Wedekind's *Lulu* were
premiered at the Almeida Theatre. His opera libretto *The Little
Prince* (music by Rachel Portman) was premiered at Houston
Grand Opera in 2003.

His writing about the theatre includes *99 Plays* – a personal
selection from Aeschylus to the present day – and *Changing
Stages*, co-written with Richard Eyre.

His Dark Materials

based on the novels by
Philip Pullman

adapted by
Nicholas Wright

NICK HERN BOOKS
London
www.nickhernbooks.co.uk

A Nick Hern Book

This stage adaptation of *His Dark Materials* first published
in Great Britain as a paperback original in 2003
by Nick Hern Books Limited, 14 Larden Road, London W3 7ST

His Dark Materials by Nicholas Wright copyright © 2003
Somerset West Limited

Afterword by Nicholas Wright copyright © 2003
Somerset West Limited

Nicholas Wright has asserted his right to be identified as
author of this work

Front cover image © Jerry Uelsmann (courtesy Laurence Miller Gallery,
New York), designed by Michael Mayhew

Typeset by Country Setting, Kingsdown, Kent, CT14 8ES
Printed and bound in Great Britain by Bookmarque, Croydon, Surrey

A CIP catalogue record for this book is available from
the British Library

ISBN 1 85459 768 X

Contents

Production Note

This adaptation was written to be played in the National
Theatre's Olivier Theatre, making maximum use of that
seldom-seen, subterranean monster, the Olivier's drum-revolve.
The demands and abilities of this mighty piece of 70's
technology are now inseparable from the script. But I like to
think that the adaptation – though it was written for a theatre
with vast resources – could have a different kind of life in
productions that have no resources at all. The fantastic
demands of Pullman's imagination can be fulfilled in many
different ways, and there's plenty in the books themselves to
stir the imagination. All that matters is that the story moves
swiftly from scene to scene.

His Dark Materials was first performed in the Olivier Theatre at the National Theatre, London, on 20 December 2003 (previews from 4 December). The cast was as follows:

Part One

Lyra Belacqua	Anna Maxwell Martin
Pantalaimon, *her daemon*	Samuel Barnett
Will Parry	Dominic Cooper

OXFORD

Master of Jordan College	Patrick Godfrey
Professor Hopcraft	Iain Mitchell
Professor of Astronomy	Andrew Westfield

Lord Asriel	Timothy Dalton
Stelmaria, *his daemon*	Emily Mytton
Thorold, *his manservant*	Nick Sampson

Mrs Coulter	Patricia Hodge
The Golden Monkey, *her daemon*	Ben Wright

Fra Pavel, *an emissary from Geneva*	Tim McMullan

Cawson, *Steward of Jordan College*	Daniel Tuite
Mrs Lonsdale, *housekeeper*	Katy Odey
Roger Parslow, *a kitchen boy*	Russell Tovey
Salcilia, *his daemon*	Helena Lymbery
Billy Costa	Jamie Harding
Tony Costa	Richard Youman

LONDON

Lord Boreal	John Carlisle
Macaw-Lady	Helen Murton
Retired General	Nick Sampson

Daisy	Helen Murton
Jessie	Katie Wimpenny
Lily	Inika Leigh Wright

Stallholder	Chris Larkin
Top-Hatted Man	Iain Mitchell
Ben, *Tony Costa's best friend*	Jason Thorpe

TROLLESUND
John Faa,
   Lord of the Western Gyptians   Stephen Greif
Farder Coram   Patrick Godfrey

Iorek Byrnison, *an armoured bear*	Danny Sapani
Bear-keeper	Akbar Kurtha
Mayor	Daniel Tuite

Kaisa, *Serafina's daemon*	Ben Whishaw
Lee Scoresby, *a balloonist*	Tim McMullan
Hester, *his daemon*	Helena Lymbery

BOLVANGAR

Sister Clara	Katy Odey
Sister Betty	Cecilia Noble
Dr West	Andrew Westfield
Dr Cade	Akbar Khurta
Dr Sargent	Iain Mitchell
Tortured Witch	Inika Leigh Wright
Clerics	Daniel Tuite
	Jason Thorpe

SVALBARD
Iofur Raknison,
   King of the armoured bears   Chris Larkin
Bear Patrol   Stephen Greif
    Iain Mitchell
    Andrew Westfield

GENEVA
President of the Consistorial Court   Stephen Greif
Brother Jasper   Ben Whishaw

LAPLAND
Serafina Pekkala,
   Queen of the Lapland witches   Niamh Cusack
Ruta Skadi,
   Queen of the Latvian witches   Cecilia Noble
Pipistrelle   Helen Murton

Caitlin	Katy Odey
Grimhild	Emily Mytton
Grendella	Katie Wimpenny
Jopari, *a Shaman*	Chris Larkin

CITTÀGAZZE
Angelica	Katie Wimpenny
Paolo	Jamie Harding
Giacomo Paradisi	Patrick Godfrey
Tullio	Ben Wright

OXFORD
Librarian	Inika Leigh Wright
Assistant	Ben Wright
Lord Boreal's butler	Andrew Westfield

Part Two

Lyra Belacqua	Anna Maxwell Martin
Pantalaimon, *her daemon*	Samuel Barnett
Will Parry	Dominic Cooper

GENEVA
President of the Consistorial Court	Stephen Greif
Brother Jasper	Ben Whishaw
Lord Boreal	John Carlisle
Dr Sargent	Iain Mitchell

OXFORD
| Mrs Coulter | Patricia Hodge |
| The Golden Monkey, *her daemon* | Ben Wright |

CITTÀGAZZE
Serafina Pekkala, Queen of the Lapland witches	Niamh Cusack
Kaisa, *her daemon*	Ben Whishaw
Pipistrelle	Helen Murton
Caitlin	Katy Odey
Grimhild	Emily Mytton
Grendella	Katie Wimpenny
Giacomo Paradisi	Patrick Godfrey
Angelica	Katie Wimpenny
Paolo	Jamie Harding

LORD ASRIEL'S FORTRESS
Lord Asriel	Timothy Dalton
Stelmaria, *his daemon*	Emily Mytton
Lord Roke, *a Gallivespian*	Tim McMullan
Officer	Russell Tovey
The Chevalier Tialys, *Gallivespian spy*	Daniel Tuite
Lady Salmakia, *Gallivespian spy*	Katie Odey

CITTÀGAZZE MOUNTAINS
Ruta Skadi, *Queen of the Latvian witches*	Cecilia Noble
Jopari	Chris Larkin
Balthamos, *an angel*	Nick Sampson
Baruch, *an angel*	Jason Thorpe
Roger	Russell Tovey

KHOLODNOYE
Iorek Byrnison, *an armoured bear*	Danny Sapani

OUTSKIRTS OF THE LAND OF THE DEAD
Perkins, *an official*	Daniel Tuite
Jeptha Jones	Andrew Westfield
Hannah, *his wife*	Helen Murton
Jones Family	Jamie Harding
	Helena Lymbery
Old Mother Jones' Death	Patrick Godfrey
Lyra's Death	Samuel Barnett
The Boatman	John Carlisle

LAND OF THE DEAD
No-name, *a harpy*	Cecilia Noble
Harpies	Inika Leigh Wright
	Helena Lymbery
Kirjava, *Will's Daemon*	Helena Lymbury

Scholars, students, stolen children, party guests, Trollesunders, witches, clerics, bears, cliff-ghasts, ghosts, Tartar guards and others played by members of the company.

Director   Nicholas Hytner
Set Designer   Giles Cadle
Costume Designer   Jon Morrell
Puppet Designer   Michael Curry
Lighting Designer   Paule Constable
Choreographer / Associate Director   Aletta Collins
Music   Jonathan Dove
Assistant to the Composer   Matthew Scott
Music Director   Steven Edis
Fight Director   Terry King
Sound Designer   Paul Groothuis

Musicians

Steven Edis (music director/keyboards); David Berry (double-bass); Fiona Clifton Welker (harp); Joy Hawley (cello); Tracy Holloway (trombone); Philip Hopkins (percussion); Colin Rae (trumpet); Nancy Ruffer (flute)

PART ONE

CHARACTERS IN PART ONE

Between the Worlds

LORD ASRIEL *and* STELMARIA
JOPARI
THOROLD, *Lord Asriel's manservant*

Lyra's World

JORDAN COLLEGE
LYRA BELACQUA *and* PANTALAIMON
ROGER PARSLOW *and* SALCILIA
THE MASTER
PROFESSOR HOPCRAFT
ASTRONOMY SCHOLAR
MRS LONSDALE
CAWSON, *a college servant*

LONDON
MRS COULTER *and* THE GOLDEN MONKEY
LORD BOREAL
MACAW-LADY
GENERAL
TOP-HATTED MAN

THE CHURCH
THE PRESIDENT
FRA PAVEL
BROTHER JASPER

GYPTIANS
LORD FAA
FARDER CORAM
TONY COSTA
BILLY COSTA
BEN

TROLLESUND
LEE SCORESBY *and* HESTER
MAYOR
BEAR-KEEPER

WITCHES
SERAFINA PEKKALA *and* KAISA
RUTA SKADI
GRIMHILD
PIPISTRELLE
CAITLIN
GRENDELLA

BOLVANGAR
DR SARGENT
DR CADE
DR WEST
NURSE

BEARS
IOREK BYRNISON
IOFUR RAKNISON

Cittàgazze

ANGELICA
PAOLO
GIACOMO PARADISI
TULLIO

Our World

WILL PARRY
LIBRARIAN
LIBRARY ASSISTANT

SCHOLARS, STUDENTS, STOLEN CHILDREN, PARTY
GUESTS, TROLLESUNDERS, WITCHES, CLERICS,
BEARS, TARTAR GUARDS, CLIFF-GHASTS *and others*

ACT ONE

Oxford / Oxford. The Botanic Gardens. Night. A tree with spreading branches. WILL and LYRA, both aged about twenty, are waiting on a wooden bench. WILL has an old green leather writing-case.

A clock strikes twelve.

LYRA. Will?

WILL. Lyra?

LYRA. This morning I half-woke up, and I felt so happy. Even before I knew what day it was. Then I remembered it was Midsummer Day. I looked at the clock and I thought, it's only sixteen hours to midnight. Sixteen hours, and I'll be sitting right next to you.

WILL. I had to scramble over the wall this time. There was a copper on duty till quarter to twelve.

LYRA. I know you're there.

Pause.

WILL. I'm wearing my one good shirt and I've cleaned my trainers. I don't usually look so smart. I'm sharing a house now with three other students, and one of them said, Hello, Will, don't tell us you've got a date at last. I said, I do, in fact. He said, oh, nice one, when do we get to meet her? I said, that might be difficult.

He laughs, then stops.

I still miss you.

PANTALAIMON. Say something.

LYRA. I will when I'm ready.

WILL. I miss Pantalaimon too. Your daemon. Your soul. I miss him as much as I miss you. Because he *is* you.

PANTALAIMON. Tell him about the college.

WILL. I know he's there. I know *you're* there. Even though you're further away from me than the furthest star . . . you're here. Right here. On the same bench. In a different world.

LYRA. I've had a very good year at college. It's like they told me, all those years ago . . . if I work very hard I can start, just start to do the things that came so naturally to me when I was a kid.

WILL. 'I spread my wings, and I brush ten million other worlds, and they know nothing of it.'

LYRA. It's different for me, from what it's like for the other students. Jordan College is new for them. They see the obvious things, like books and towers and ancient stones. I see the place where I grew up. I see Mrs Lonsdale, who was meant to look after me and keep me tidy . . .

MRS LONSDALE *is there to change* LYRA*'s clothes.*

MRS LONSDALE. Just what do you think you're wearing, Miss Lyra?

LYRA. . . . and the mouse-holes and the secret doorways, and the hiding-places. And the mouldy old scholars with their flapping gowns. I see Roger, like he was on the day I met him. I was twelve. Me and the other college kids had been fighting the kids from town. Then we all joined up to fight the brick-burners' kids down by the clay-pits. And then we remembered it was the horse-fair week . . . so we all rushed down to the river to fight the gyptian kids. I was fighting Billy Costa.

LYRA*'s Oxford.* WILL *and his world disappear.* LYRA *is twelve. Assorted* KIDS *are yelling at the* GYPTIAN KIDS:

Oi! Gyppoes!

Water rats!

Fortune-tellers!

Tea-leaves!

Want any knives sharpened?

Any old iron!

GYPTIAN KIDS *and other* KIDS *fight.* LYRA *gets* BILLY COSTA *down on the ground in a headlock. The others clear.*

LYRA. Give up, Billy?

BILLY. No!

LYRA. Now?

BILLY. No!

LYRA. What about now?

BILLY. Yeah! Get off.

They stand.

How'd you do that?

LYRA. It's a headlock. Look, I'll show you.

BILLY. Leave off!

BILLY*'s brother* TONY *appears.*

TONY. Oi, Billy! Our ma says, get back home this minute or she'll give you a clip.

LYRA. Hello, Tony.

TONY. Don't you 'hello' me, you horrible little tyke. Wasn't it you throwing mud at our boat just now?

LYRA. That weren't me. It was some other kids. They come down from Abingdon in a special coach . . . all painted black, with a skeleton driving. And he saw your boat, and he pointed his bony finger . . .

TONY. Oh aye. Lyra the liar. En't that what they call you? Go on, get back home. It'll be dark before you know it, and then the you-know-whats'll get you. Come on, Billy.

He and BILLY *go.* LYRA *stays, dejected.* ROGER *runs on.*

ROGER. Where's the fighting?

LYRA. You missed it.

ROGER. Who won?

LYRA. Dunno. Don't matter either. See yer, whoever you are.

ROGER. See yer.

They turn to go.

PANTALAIMON. I'm Pantalaimon.

SALCILIA. I'm Salcilia.

PANTALAIMON. I en't seen you before.

SALCILIA. That's 'cause we only just arrived from London.

The DAEMONS *approach each other.* LYRA *and* ROGER *look at them in surprise.*

ROGER. That's funny.

LYRA. They wanna be friends.

ROGER. That could be. My mum always says, you know at once when you like somebody. An' I like you. I'm Roger. Roger Parslow. My dad's the new head gardener at Gabriel College, an' me mum's a cook an' I'm gonna be a kitchen-boy.

LYRA. I'm Lyra Belacqua an' I'm at Jordan. I don't work there or nothing. I just play around.

ROGER. Jordan's bigger'n Gabriel, en't it?

LYRA. It's bigger an' richer an' ever so much more important. You wanna see it?

ROGER. Yeah, don't mind.

LYRA. Come on then.

They walk on.

ROGER. Where's *your* mum an' dad?

LYRA. En't got none. I'm nearly an orphan.

ROGER. You can't be *nearly* an orphan.

LYRA. You can if you're me. I got an uncle, and he's famous.

ROGER. Bet I never heard of 'im.

LYRA. Bet you have.

ROGER. So what's his name?

LYRA. Lord Asriel.

ROGER. *Him*? What, the explorer an' all?

LYRA. That's right.

ROGER. Well that *is* famous. What's he like?

LYRA. He's old, dead old, like forty at least. His daemon's a snow-leopard. And Lord Asriel's *ferocious*. There was some Tartars caught him once, and they tied him up, and one of 'em was just gonna cut his guts out, and Lord Asriel looked at him – just looked, like that – and he dropped down dead.

PANTALAIMON. Lyra the liar!

LYRA. It was summat like that.

They have arrived at Jordan College.

Look, that's a scholar, and the rest are students.

A black-robed SCHOLAR *is demonstrating a revolving model of the solar system to a group of* STUDENTS. *He indicates the five planets.*

ASTRONOMY SCHOLAR. Hermes, Aphrodite, Earth, Ares, Zeus, Poseidon. All revolving, as the Church has at last acknowledged, around the sun.

He moves on, and another scholar – PROFESSOR HOPCRAFT *– appears. He's lecturing to a group of* STUDENTS.

LYRA. This one don't like me.

HOPCRAFT. Man. And Daemon. What is the force between them?

The STUDENTS *write, muttering, 'What is the force . . . ?'*

If the man is an adult, his daemon cannot, of course, transform its shape, as that of a child can do.

PANTALAIMON *and* SALCILIA *change shape.*

PANTALAIMON. Like this.

SALCILIA. Or this.

LYRA. Stop showing off.

They laugh. HOPCRAFT *glares at them.*

HOPCRAFT. Why, if I moved the man away from his daemon, would he experience, first, discomfort . . . then pain . . . then a grinding sense of loss and finally death? This is one of creation's ultimate mysteries. And here is another. Why is it unthinkable that I could touch his daemon?

PANTALAIMON. Touch another person's daemon!

SALCILIA. That's revolting!

THE MASTER *appears with* FRA PAVEL.

MASTER. Professor Hopcraft, may I disturb you?

LYRA. That's the Master of the College.

ROGER. Who's that snakey feller who's pickin' his nose?

LYRA. That's Fra Pavel. He comes to look at me twice a year and asks me questions.

MASTER (*to* FRA PAVEL). May I present our new head of experimental theology? (*To* HOPCRAFT.) Fra Pavel arrived this morning from Geneva, from the Consistorial Court of Discipline.

HOPCRAFT (*to* FRA PAVEL). Your visit comes none too soon, your reverence. I'm all for academic freedom, but some of the views that I've been hearing bandied around the Common Room are most alarming.

FRA PAVEL. May I suggest that you provide me with the names of the staff involved?

HOPCRAFT. I shall, I shall, it will be an honour.

To his STUDENTS:

Gentlemen, tutorial over. I've a paper to write.

He and the STUDENTS *go.* THE MASTER *has seen*
LYRA.

MASTER. Lyra, come here.

LYRA *approaches.*

FRA PAVEL. Good evening, Lyra.

LYRA (*guarded*). 'Ello.

FRA PAVEL. Are you still happy at Jordan College?

LYRA. Sort of.

FRA PAVEL. Do you learn your lessons? Do you say your
prayers to the Authority?

LYRA. Mm hm.

FRA PAVEL. And have you decided what you will do, once
you've grown up and your daemon is settled?

LYRA. I'll go exploring with Lord Asriel. He's gonna take
me up the Amazon river, or into the desert, or the Arctic
Circle . . .

FRA PAVEL (*to* THE MASTER). Is this true?

MASTER. No, not at all. You surely remember her weakness
for fantastic stories. Your uncle is far too busy to see you
when he comes to Jordan College, isn't he, Lyra?

LYRA. But he's coming on Wednesday week. Mrs Lonsdale
told me. And he'll see me then, I'm gonna make sure he
does. I'll follow him round, till . . .

MASTER. He will be here for one night only, Lyra. If you . . .

FRA PAVEL (*to* LYRA). Play with your friend.

LYRA *goes. Icily:*

Why was I not informed of Lord Asriel's visit?

MASTER. I would have warned you, but . . . please let me finish. Lord Asriel has offered to show us the findings of his latest expedition to the Arctic. Some of the scholars are most enthusiastic. Others, of course, are as shocked as you. What can I do? I try to steer a moderate course, but . . .

FRA PAVEL. There *is* no moderate course. There's only good and evil.

MASTER. But surely . . .

FRA PAVEL. You're either for the Church or you're against it. Don't you *see* that? Don't you know what's happening outside your smug little ivory tower? Fears of war. Rebellion. Dissent, confusion, schism, doubt. All fuelled by the mad ambitions of Lord Asriel and the complacency of academics like yourself.

MASTER. Then I shall follow your instructions. Which are what, exactly?

FRA PAVEL. Since that heretic has been foolish enough to place himself in your hands, you must take advantage of it. You must render him harmless, by the most extreme of measures. Is that agreed?

MASTER. No, certainly not! Or only if . . . though, on the other hand . . . I'll do as you say. But under protest.

FRA PAVEL. Let's walk on.

They do.

Lyra has changed. I see in her, both the child she is, and the woman she will become.

MASTER. Is anything wrong with that?

FRA PAVEL (*with great meaning*). Time will tell.

They go.

Two weeks later. Oxford. Evening. SCHOLARS *appear, and continue to assemble.* LYRA *and* ROGER *are there, with their* DAEMONS.

1ST SCHOLAR (*to* LYRA). Off the quad! Off the quad!

They back off, but stay watching. To his fellow SCHOLARS:

He's here! Look, there's his zeppelin!

They all look up.

2ND SCHOLAR. I do believe he's mooring it to the roof of the chapel.

3RD SCHOLAR. Disgraceful!

5TH SCHOLAR. Rather amusing, though!

4TH SCHOLAR (*who is very old*). Is something happening?

1ST SCHOLAR. Yes, Lord Asriel's just arrived.

4TH SCHOLAR. What did he say? No, not that ear, the other one.

Someone explains, as:

1ST SCHOLAR. We'll exchange a few polite formalities, and then we'll take him through to dinner in the Great Hall.

HOPCRAFT *has arrived.*

HOPCRAFT. Oh gentlemen, what's going on? It's not a *welcoming* party, surely?

3RD SCHOLAR. We mustn't let Lord Asriel think that we approve of him.

1ST SCHOLAR. Well some of us do.

Disagreement breaks out, as:

5TH SCHOLAR. The Master's gone to greet him, so he can't be totally in disgrace.

THOROLD *appears, accompanied by* CAWSON, *a college servant, who is carrying equipment.*

There's his manservant.

SEVERAL. Welcome, Thorold!

THOROLD. Evening, gentlemen.

1ST SCHOLAR. The lecture is in the Retiring Room. Through that archway, round the chapel and . . .

THOROLD. I en't forgotten my way, sir. (*To* CAWSON.) Mind that box, Mr. Cawson, there's glass inside it.

He goes.

1ST SCHOLAR. It seems that Lord Asriel is going to give us a magic-lantern show.

HOPCRAFT. Is he? Really? Doesn't that smack of entertainment?

THE MASTER *appears.*

MASTER. Our guest is here.

LORD ASRIEL *enters with his snow-leopard daemon,* STELMARIA. *There's a ripple of applause from the* SCHOLARS. *He shakes their hands as they exchange greetings.* LYRA *tries to attract his attention, but is effortlessly shunted off by the* SCHOLARS, *who appear used to her intrusions.*

LORD ASRIEL (*to a* SCHOLAR). Professor Tonkin, I hear your book's been a great success. (*To another.*) Congratulations on your professorship, Richard. (*To* HOPCRAFT.) You must be Professor Hopcraft. May I just say how much I admire your writing?

HOPCRAFT (*flattered*). Oh, you've read it? Well I'm flattered. Though I doubt that . . .

MASTER. Shall we go to the dining-hall, my lord?

They leave. LYRA *and* ROGER *are there: they've been watching.*

ROGER. He's awesome.

She starts to go.

Hey, where you goin'?

LYRA. Where d'you think? We're gonna sneak into the Retiring Room while they're still having their dinner.

PANTALAIMON. Lyra, we can't! It en't just any old room.

SALCILIA. Kids can't go in there, and nor can women.

PANTALAIMON. Yeah, and it's probably haunted.

LYRA. Good, that settles it. Come on Rodge, I know a secret
way.

The Retiring Room appears. It's cavernous and reverential.
THOROLD *and* CAWSON *are there,* CAWSON *putting in
place a tray with a glass and a decanter of wine.*

CAWSON. The 1898, this is. The Keeper of Wine was greatly
taken aback, but the Master was most particular.

THOROLD. Lord Asriel will appreciate that. He's very partial
to that year.

They go. LYRA *and* ROGER *creep out of a secret door and
look round.*

LYRA. Yeah.

ROGER. It's spooky all right.

PANTALAIMON. This is a bad idea.

ROGER *finds projection equipment laid out. Picks up a
slide.*

ROGER. 'Ere, look.

SALCILIA. Don't touch it!

ROGER. I won't break it.

He holds a slide up to the light.

This is pretty. Lyra, come an' see what I found.

LYRA. I wanna look at them paintings. All the Masters with
their daemons.

PANTALAIMON. Now that *is* interesting.

They look.

LYRA. He's got a falcon-daemon.

PANTALAIMON. He's got a magpie.

LYRA. That one's got an owl. He must have been specially clever.

A bell is heard.

They've finished their dinner. Let's go back in there. Pan, Salcilia, change into something small.

They hide. THE MASTER *comes in furtively.* LYRA, ROGER *and their* DAEMONS *watch as, having satisfied himself that the room is empty,* THE MASTER *takes a small bottle from his pocket and empties it into the decanter. He looks round once more, and goes.* LYRA *and the others look out.*

He poisoned the wine!

ROGER. How d'you know it's poison?

LYRA. It must be. Why else did he look around like that, all furtive-like?

PANTALAIMON. We can't make a fuss, or we'll get into trouble.

LYRA. I can't let my uncle be murdered, Pan!

ROGER. Shuddup! He's here!

LORD ASRIEL *comes in with* STELMARIA *and* THOROLD, *who adjusts the projection equipment.* LYRA, ROGER *and their* DAEMONS *watch.*

LORD ASRIEL. Is the equipment all set up?

THOROLD. It is, sir.

LORD ASRIEL. Excellent. The sooner I can get out of this place, the better.

CAWSON *comes in with a cup of coffee on a tray.*

CAWSON. Good evening, my lord.

LORD ASRIEL. Good evening, Cawson. Is that the Tokay I can see on the table?

CAWSON. It is, sir. There are only three bottles left in the cellars. The Master ordered it decanted especially for you.

LORD ASRIEL. You may go.

CAWSON goes. LORD ASRIEL goes to pour wine. LYRA watches in great suspense.

Smell the air. Must, fust and dry bones. Nothing has changed. Nothing is new. I'd like to smash those windows and let some air in.

STELMARIA. You're tired. You ought to be resting.

LORD ASRIEL. I know, I know. And I ought to have changed my clothes. There's probably some ancient etiquette that allows them to fine me half a swan and a bottle of claret for being improperly dressed.

He is about to drink.

LYRA. No!

LORD ASRIEL. Who's that?

LYRA. Don't drink it!

She scrambles forward to snatch the glass from his hand.

LORD ASRIEL. Lyra! What are you doing in here?

LYRA. Throw it away! It's poisoned.

LORD ASRIEL. What did you say?

LYRA. I saw the Master pouring something into it.

LORD ASRIEL. The *Master*?

LYRA. Yeah. I was hiding in there, an' . . .

LORD ASRIEL sees ROGER.

LORD ASRIEL. Who's that?

LYRA. That's Roger. He's my best friend. 'Ere, Rodge . . . !

ROGER comes out.

LORD ASRIEL (*to* ROGER). Stay where you are, young man. One bothersome child is quite enough.

To LYRA:

Why were you hiding?

LYRA. I wanted to see you. I wanted to ask you when you'd take me to the Arctic, so I'd . . .

LORD ASRIEL. Don't be ridiculous. You're a child.

LYRA. But . . .

LORD ASRIEL. Lyra, I haven't got time to argue. You talk about my new expedition. I can't pay for my new expedition. I'm trying to get the college to pay, and they don't know that yet. Go away. No, stop. Let me look at you.

He looks at her.

You seem healthy enough. Show me your hands.

She does.

Disgusting.

THOROLD *is at the door.*

THOROLD. The scholars are here, my lord.

LORD ASRIEL (*to* LYRA). Here are five gold dollars. Get back where you were. Go on!

She hides. THE MASTER *comes in, followed by* SCHOLARS. *He looks in shock at* LORD ASRIEL, *then at the decanter.*

Wrong vintage, Master. Will you begin?

MASTER. I will . . . but I seem to have lost my notes.

He improvises to the assembly:

Gentlemen, in these difficult times, we seldom enjoy the privilege of controversy. And controversy is what Lord Asriel will surely provide us with this evening. But let us remember that it is only his high position that allows him to speak so freely. We humble scholars must speak and think as the Church allows us. It is the Church alone which knows the mind of the eternal source of truth, the omnipotent power, the Authority. Praise be to him.

All except LORD ASRIEL *make the sacred sign of the Authority.*

ALL. Praise be to him.

MASTER. Lord Asriel?

LORD ASRIEL. Thorold, turn down the lamp.

THOROLD *does so and goes.*

I set out for the Arctic twelve months ago, on what I described as a diplomatic mission to the King of Lapland. My real aim was very different. It was to follow the steps of a certain spirit-diviner, an occultist, a *shaman* as he's known to the Northern tribesmen. His name is Jopari.

A slide comes up of JOPARI *standing in the moonlight in the snow, beside a hut, with one hand raised.*

Here he stands, one hand raised up in greeting. The photogram I shall show you next was taken from the same position a moment later, by a secret process that Jopari taught me.

A slide comes up of the same scene, but with JOPARI *bathed in unearthly light, with a fountain of sparks streaming from – or to – his raised hand. The* SCHOLARS *murmur to each other in surprise.*

The process uses as emulsion, an amber liquid that reveals the presence of that mysterious substance . . . or power . . . or essence . . . that all of us know about, and that no-one truly understands. It is that flood of elementary particles that we call Dust.

Sensation. HOPCRAFT *springs up.*

HOPCRAFT. I understood that talk about Dust was not allowed. What is Fra Pavel's view?

MASTER. Fra Pavel is in Geneva. But he told me before he left, that we should watch our tongues.

HOPCRAFT. Well there you are! We could all be in very deep water indeed, unless we . . .

LORD ASRIEL *loses his temper.*

LORD ASRIEL. Gentlemen, I risked my life to take these photograms. Look at the picture! What does it show us? Dust is bathing the man in radiance. Just as it does to all of us, every moment of our adult lives. But with us, that radiance is invisible. Here, for the first time in human history, we can see it. Here at last we have a clue to the questions that have baffled us ever since Dust was named. Where does it come from? The picture seems to show it streaming down from the sky. Is that the answer? But why has it collected in such quantity around Jopari? Has it *chosen* him? Has Dust an intelligence?

Animated conversation breaks out between the SCHOLARS.

MASTER. Gentlemen, please!

LORD ASRIEL. All this is a mere introduction to my main discovery. Here is a slide of the Aurora Borealis.

A slide comes up of the Aurora Borealis.

4TH SCHOLAR. Forgive my ignorance, but if I ever knew what the Aurora was, I have forgotten. Is it the Northern Lights?

LORD ASRIEL. It is. The picture you're looking at was taken in the old-fashioned way. But by using Jopari's process, I revealed something I could hardly believe myself.

A second slide appears, looking basically the same as the previous one.

3RD SCHOLAR. It's just the same.

1ST SCHOLAR. No . . . there's something different in the centre.

2ND SCHOLAR. Lord Asriel, could you enlarge it, please?

LORD ASRIEL *does. A city appears in the Aurora.*

LORD ASRIEL. We see a city suspended in the air. Towers, domes, walls, buildings, streets, even a line of palm trees . . . all visible through the boundaries of the world we know.

5TH SCHOLAR. Are you saying this city is outside our world?

1ST SCHOLAR. It must be.

2ND SCHOLAR. There aren't any palm trees in *our* Arctic.

LORD ASRIEL. Exactly. In searching for Dust, I discovered
a different world! Think what that means. If Dust can travel
from world to world, then so can light. If light can travel,
then so can we. The doors are open to us. The chains are
broken. We can question everything we've been taught.
We can challenge every dreary, grey belief that we've had
dinned into our skulls. Our reach is infinite, and I shall
prove it. I shall go back to the Arctic. I'll find the Aurora.
I'll build a pathway through its heart into this different
world, and I'll cross into it! Will the college support me?

HOPCRAFT. Certainly not! This is blatant support for a
certain theory . . .

5TH SCHOLAR. What theory, Professor Hopcraft?

HOPCRAFT. I mean the multi-world theory as you, Professor
Chalker, very well know!

1ST SCHOLAR. I'd like to propose that we offer Lord Asriel
a handsome subvention from the College funds!

Cries of 'Hear, hear!' THE MASTER *springs up.*

MASTER. This is going too far!

LORD ASRIEL. Put it to the vote!

5TH SCHOLAR. All those in favour?

Cries of 'Aye'!

3RD SCHOLAR. All those against?

A few 'No!'s

MASTER (*in despair*). The motion is carried.

The meeting erupts into pandemonium:

ANTI. You're all quite mad. The Church will make a stink and
close down our research programmes. / Lord Asriel has
been a menace to Jordan College ever since I knew him as

an undergraduate. / We ought to be fighting Dust, not taking pictures of it. / Who says those photograms are real? They don't look real to me. / They could all be a fake. (*etc.*)

PRO. Excellent! Good! We've been sorely lacking in circumstantial evidence, and we all know why that is, but . . . / I've known for *years* and *years* that the multi-world theory is solid fact but . . . / Well the camera doesn't lie. It doesn't. Really it doesn't. I mean, we've seen the palm trees and the city and all the rest of it . . . / My undergraduates think I'm a boring old fossil because I cannot admit the truth. / *What* did you say? *What* did you say? (*etc.*)

Six weeks later. Jordan College. Outside, on a summer afternoon. LYRA, ROGER, PANTALAIMON *and* SALCILIA. LYRA *is downcast.*

LYRA. It's six weeks gone since he went to the Arctic, an' he en't never wrote nor nothing.

ROGER. I thought you said he never does.

LYRA. It's different now. I saved his life. You'd think a postcard wouldn't be too much bother.

PANTALAIMON. Or a carrier-pigeon.

ROGER. It were something though, weren't it? All them scholars standing on chairs an' shouting' . . .

LYRA. . . . and the man with his hand held up. You know what, Rodge?

ROGER. No, what?

LYRA. If I go to the Arctic . . . *when* I go . . . I'm gonna take you with me.

ROGER. I never thought no different.

MRS LONSDALE *appears.*

MRS LONSDALE. There you are. Lyra, you're to come with me and visit the Master. No time to wash, we'll have to make do with hankie and spit.

She does.

LYRA. I don't wanna see him!

ROGER. Can't you say you couldn't find her?

MRS LONSDALE. What are you talking about, you two? Don't say you're frightened of the Master. (*To* LYRA.) Stand still. And don't ever again let me find you out and about without no grown-ups. It's not safe any more. There's kids being stolen in broad daylight, not but what anyone knows who's taking 'em.

LYRA. It's the Gobblers take 'em.

MRS LONSDALE. Yes, but who's the Gobblers? That's the question.

ROGER. My dad says there en't no Gobblers. He says it's all got up by the papers.

MRS LONSDALE. Well he's wrong, quite wrong. There's Gobblers all over the country. There, that's better.

They walk on.

LYRA. But there en't none in Oxford, is there, Mrs Lonsdale?

MRS LONSDALE. I'm afraid there is. I didn't want to upset you, but you'll hear about it soon enough. Young Billy Costa's gone.

LYRA *is shocked.*

LYRA. What, Billy?

ROGER. How did it happen?

MRS LONSDALE. It was just like *that*. He was holding a horse for his brother Tony, and Tony took his eye off him just for a minute, and when he looked back, Billy had vanished.

LYRA. Isn't nobody gonna look for him?

MRS LONSDALE. The gyptians may, but us landlopers won't be bothering, sad to say. Here we are.

They have arrived at THE MASTER*'s study.*

ROGER. Don't drink nothing he gives you.

LYRA. Yeah, and you wait outside and listen, and if I scream
for help, you gotta come running in.

THE MASTER*'s study.* MRS LONSDALE *knocks on the door.*

MASTER. Come in.

LYRA *and* MRS LONSDALE *go in.* THE MASTER *is
there.*

MRS LONSDALE. No-one keeping an eye on 'er, and the
Gobblers in Oxford too.

MASTER. Thank you, Mrs Lonsdale.

She goes.

Sit down, Lyra.

LYRA *does.*

You have been in the care of Jordan College for twelve
years now, ever since you were brought here as a baby.
We are fond of you, you've never been a bad child and
you've been happy, I think, in your own way. But that part
of your life has ended.

LYRA. What do you mean?

MASTER. A very well-known and distinguished person has
offered to take you away.

LYRA. You mean Lord Asriel?

MASTER. No! Lord Asriel cannot communicate with anyone.

LYRA. Is he dead?

MASTER. No, certainly not. He went to the Arctic, as you
know, and I have reason to believe he's safe. Now, as for
you. There is a friend of the college, a wealthy widow, who
has offered to take you to live with her in London.

LYRA. I don't want no bloody widow! I wanna stay here!

MASTER. Lyra . . .

MRS COULTER. May I speak to her?

> MRS COULTER *appears: a sophisticated and very attractive woman wearing a long yellow-red fox-fur coat. Her* DAEMON *is a golden monkey.*

MASTER. Certainly, Mrs Coulter. This is Lyra.

> MRS COULTER *looks at her.*

LYRA. What you lookin' at?

MRS COULTER. You. I haven't seen you since . . . well, ever. And you're just as they described you . . . Do you like chocolatl? I think I have some in my bag.

> LYRA *receives the chocolatl with a show of indifference.*

I know how nervous you must be feeling. I'm a little nervous myself, believe it or not. But we'll soon get to know each other. We'll be friends.

LYRA. I've got a friend. I play with him all the time. An' . . .

MRS COULTER. Lyra, don't you think you're just a little too old for rough-and-tumble games with children from a different background? You'll be a young woman soon, and you could be a very pretty one. Wouldn't you like that?

LYRA. What, just being pretty all day?

MRS COULTER. Oh, more than that. You'll be my personal assistant.

MASTER. Mrs Coulter is the Chief Executive Officer of a very significant organisation.

LYRA. What's it called?

MRS COULTER. It's called the General Oblation Board. It finds out all about Dust. Have you heard about Dust?

> LYRA *glances at* THE MASTER.

LYRA. I have, yeah . . . but I thought we wasn't supposed to talk about it.

MRS COULTER. You can if you have permission. And the Church has given the General Oblation Board its total backing. I shall want you to meet my clients, keep my appointment book . . . and there'll be travel, of course.

LYRA. Where to?

MRS COULTER. The Arctic, mostly. I have some very interesting projects there. We'll have to fly by zeppelin . . . watching the icebergs floating past below us . . . or would that be too adventurous for you?

LYRA. No, but . . . No, it wouldn't.

MRS COULTER. And once we get there, there'll be lots of dangerous creatures . . . witches, armoured bears . . . and hungry cliff-ghasts . . . you won't like *that*, I suppose . . .

LYRA. I might not mind.

MRS COULTER. And isn't there someone very special in the Arctic? Someone you'd like to see, who I could take you to?

LYRA. Do you know Lord Asriel?

MRS COULTER. I know him *very well*. So what do you say?

MASTER. The truth is, Lyra, that neither you nor I can choose where we wish to go. We are moved by tides much fiercer than you can imagine, and they sweep us all into the current.

MRS COULTER. Thank you, Master, you've been extremely helpful. I shall inform Geneva. Lyra, my dear, good night. We'll leave in the morning.

She hugs LYRA.

We're going to have such fun!

She goes. LYRA *stands.*

MASTER. One moment, Lyra. Were you by any chance concealed in the Retiring Room, the night Lord Asriel spoke to the Scholars?

LYRA. I might have been.

MASTER. So you have reason to mistrust me?

LYRA. Yeah, I do.

MASTER. You must understand, a man in my position has to commit some evil from time to time, to prevent some greater harm. But one can try to make up for it. There will be dangers where you are going. You will need protection. I am giving you this.

He produces a small package wrapped in black velvet. Unwraps it, to reveal a beautiful, golden compass-like mechanism. LYRA *looks at it.*

LYRA. What is it?

MASTER. It is an alethiometer. It was constructed in Prague three hundred years ago. Only six were ever made, and even fewer survive. Lord Asriel presented this one to the college when he was young.

LYRA. What does it do?

MASTER. It tells the truth. But it does so in a way so deep and so mysterious that adults need a whole library of reference books to understand it.

LYRA. What about children?

MASTER. Who can say? Innocence can be wiser than experience. If you could read it, Lyra, even if only a very little, it would be the greatest treasure you ever possessed. Respect it. Keep it safe. Tell no-one you have it.

LYRA. Not even Mrs Coulter?

MASTER. *Especially* not Mrs Coulter. Now take it and go.

LYRA *takes the alethiometer and goes into the night outside.*

LYRA. Roger! Roger!

MRS LONSDALE *appears, carrying a lantern.*

Oh, Mrs Lonsdale. Have you seen Roger?

MRS LONSDALE. No, I haven't. Nobody has. They can't find him anywhere.

LYRA. What?

MRS LONSDALE. He was standing here. Right here. I told him he ought to go home. And now the Gobblers have taken him. Oh, that stupid, stupid boy!

LYRA. How can you say that? Don't you care about Roger?

MRS LONSDALE. People care about things in different ways, Miss Lyra. We don't all show it. Roger's my nephew.

LYRA. I didn't know.

MRS LONSDALE. You didn't know because you never asked. He was waiting for *you*.

She moves away, peering into the darkness.

LYRA. He's gone.

PANTALAIMON. Salcilia too.

LYRA. Can you feel it, Pan? It's like I'm only half of meself, and the other half's just . . . not there.

PANTALAIMON. You still got me.

LYRA. Yeah.

She hugs PANTALAIMON.

I'd die if I didn't. And you know what, Pan? Whatever they've done to Roger, wherever they've taken him . . . we're gonna find him. We're gonna rescue him. I swear it.

London. A bleak collection-point. A brazier is burning. CHILDREN are there, including BILLY COSTA, who is playing with a toy train. An old SERVANT hands round mugs of hot chocolatl. ROGER appears.

ROGER. 'Ello.

SEVERAL. 'Ello.

BILLY. 'Ello Rodge. Come an' sit down. (*To the* CHILD *beside him.*) Move up, willya?

He catches the SERVANT*'s eye and points to* ROGER.

Oi, Miss. Don't forget the new boy.

ROGER *sits by him. The* SERVANT *gives* ROGER *a mugful of chocalatl. Meanwhile:*

'Ere, Ratter. You know Roger. Say 'ello.

RATTER, *his daemon, turns away.*

Nah, she's gloomy today.

ROGER. Billy . . .

BILLY. Yeah?

ROGER. . . . 'Ave we been taken by the Gobblers?

The CHILDREN *laugh.*

BILLY. Sure 'ave, mate.

ROGER. What they gonna do to us?

BILLY. Nothin' nasty.

PLUMP GIRL. We all had'ta write letters to our mums and dads. In case they're worried about us, know what I mean?

RED-HAIRED GIRL. Catch mine getting worried.

ROGER. Is it all right, then? Being a Gobbler-victim?

PLUMP GIRL. Yeah, it's nice.

RED-HAIRED GIRL. We're getting' to like it, en't we, Lily?

DARK-HAIRED GIRL. We're goin' on a boat.

ROGER. A *boat*? Where to?

DARK-HAIRED GIRL. Dunno, but it's gotta be more excitin' than being at 'ome.

RED-HAIRED GIRL. I hope it's somewhere 'ot.

DARK-HAIRED GIRL. Yeah, with long white beaches.

RED-HAIRED GIRL. Or a swimmin' pool!

They all laugh.

PLUMP GIRL. Ssh! Look be'ind you.

She indicates THE GOLDEN MONKEY, *who is now lurking.* MRS COULTER *appears.*

MRS COULTER. Have you finished your letters?

ALL. Yes, miss.

MRS COULTER. Hold them out.

They do, and she collects them.

Have you all been given a suitcase?

ALL. Yes, miss.

MRS COULTER. And your pyjamas? Nighties? Toothbrushes?

ALL. Yes, miss!

MRS COULTER. And who likes chocolatl?

ALL. Me! Me!

MRS COULTER. Well, I happen to know that they'll be handing some out to you the minute you get on board.

ALL. Hooray!

THE GOLDEN MONKEY *indicates* ROGER.

MRS COULTER. Oh dear, you didn't have time to write. But I can give your mother a message.

ROGER. Will you tell her . . .

MRS COULTER. Yes?

ROGER. . . . . to feed my budgie?

MRS COULTER. Isn't there something more important?

ROGER. Just say I love her.

MRS COULTER. She'll be so happy to hear that!

A ship's hooter blows. A door opens and a SEA-CAPTAIN *appears. The* CHILDREN *file out.*

Form a line . . . that's right . . . There'll be a nurse to look after you . . . make sure you tell her if you're feeling sea-sick . . . Ladies first, Billy . . . No pushing each other on the gangplank. Goodbye!

The last CHILDREN *to leave wave and call 'Goodbye'. To the* MONKEY:

Get rid of these.

She gives the letters to THE GOLDEN MONKEY *and leaves. He throws the letters into the brazier and watches them burn.*

MRS COULTER'*s living-room.* LYRA, *prettily dressed, is looking at herself in a mirror.*

LYRA (*to* PANTALAIMON). I en't never been pretty before. Never in all my life. I en't never had my hair done proper, and my nails all pink and polished.

PANTALAIMON. She's just turning you into a pet.

LYRA. She loves me, though, I'm sure she does. She sits on the end of my bed when she thinks I'm asleep, and she looks at me, so sad, with those big dark eyes.

PANTALAIMON. If she's so good, then why's she got such a horrible, evil daemon?

LYRA. I dunno. It's like she's evil and good all at the same time.

She takes out the alethiometer.

PANTALAIMON. What you doin'?

LYRA. I'm gonna have one more go at finding Roger before she comes barging in. I been thinking. If I point the needles at the pictures round the outside . . . maybe that's part of asking the question.

PANTALAIMON *looks.*

PANTALAIMON. Point one of 'em at the moon.

LYRA. Why the moon?

PANTALAIMON. Because it disappears like Roger did.

LYRA. Yeah, right. And the horse, for travel. And . . . what stands for 'Roger'?

PANTALAIMON. Something to do with 'friend'.

LYRA. The dolphin, 'cause dolphins are friendly.

The needles are all in place.

PANTALAIMON. Go on.

LYRA. 'Where's Roger?'

They watch.

PANTALAIMON. The big needle's moving.

LYRA. Yeah, but it's not saying nothing, is it? It's just swinging around any old how.

Louder:

'Where's Roger?' Oh Pan, it's stopped!

PANTALAIMON. Look out.

MRS COULTER *comes in with a vase of flowers.* LYRA *sneaks the alethiometer back into her shoulder-bag.*

MRS COULTER. Lyra dear, you haven't been out, I hope?

LYRA. No, I been in all day.

MRS COULTER. I know I'm always saying this, and I'm sure you must find it very boring of me, but if you want to go out, you must do so with me or . . .

LYRA / MRS COULTER. . . . with one of the servants.

MRS COULTER. Exactly.

She re-arranges the flowers.

Now you are quite clear about what I want you to do at the party this evening?

LYRA. I en't forgo'en.

MRS COULTER. *Haven't* forgotten! Sound those 't's. 'T', 't', 't'. I want you to circulate with the canapés and make agreeable conversation. There'll be some very influential people here . . . people in government and potential funders and opinion-formers . . . and it's important to me that you live up to their expectations.

LYRA. They don't know nothin' about me.

MRS COULTER. One can be better known than one is aware of, Lyra. Let me look at you.

She does.

Not bad. Not bad at all. But not the shoulder-bag, of course. Will you take it off, please?

THE GOLDEN MONKEY *paws the shoulder-bag.*

LYRA. But I really like it. It's the only thing I've got that belongs to me.

MRS COULTER. Lyra, it looks absurd to wear a shoulder-bag in one's own home. Take it off!

LYRA. No!

She stamps her foot.

MRS COULTER. I'll ask you one more time. Take off that bag. And never stamp your foot again, either in my sight or out of it.

LYRA *picks up* PANTALAIMON *and turns to go.*

LYRA. Come on, Pan.

THE GOLDEN MONKEY *springs on to* PANTALAIMON, *pinning him to the ground.* LYRA *feels pain.*

Stop hurting us! Please!

MRS COULTER *calmly re-arranges the flowers.*

MRS COULTER. I think you'll find that once you remove the bag, he'll let you go.

LYRA *gives her the bag.* THE GOLDEN MONKEY *releases* PANTALAIMON.

Thank you. Now there's something I want to do.

She produces a pair of nail-scissors.

Do you see this locket around my neck? There's nothing inside. It's like an empty heart just waiting to be filled. I'm going to cut off a lock of your hair.

She cuts off a lock of LYRA*'s hair and places it in the locket.*

There. Now kiss me.

LYRA *does.*

Have the caterers brought enough ice, do you think? Warm drinks are *horrid.*

She moves away. LYRA *holds* PANTALAIMON *close.*

PANTALAIMON. She's evil all through.

LYRA. I hate her!

GUESTS *arrive and the room is full.* LYRA *and* PANTALAIMON *circulate with a tray of canapés. They approach a* LADY *with a* MACAW-DAEMON, *who is talking to the* 2ND GUEST.

Can I give you a canopy, miss?

MACAW-LADY. Thank you, my dear. So few young gels are helpful to their mothers these days.

LYRA. Oh, Mrs Coulter's not my mother. I'm her assistant.

MACAW-LADY (*archly*). Really?

2ND GUEST. Then who *are* your family?

LYRA. Well, my parents died in an airship accident when I was a baby. But my uncle is Lord Asriel.

MACAW-LADY. Oh, your *uncle*, is he?

She and the 2ND GUEST *laugh and turn away.*

PANTALAIMON. 'Oh, your *uncle*, is he?'

LYRA. Ssh.

PANTALAIMON. She's like that parrot of hers.

They pass another group, which includes a retired
GENERAL.

1ST GUEST. Oh yes, there'll certainly be a war. We're simply
marking time until our so-called allies have made their
minds up.

GENERAL. Well you can take it from me, young man, if I
were still in command I'd swap the lot of them for a sturdy
brigade of armoured bears.

1ST GUEST. Would you, General? Aren't they notoriously
unreliable?

GENERAL. Oh good Lord, no. As long as you've paid your
bear, he'll stick to you thick and thin, that's my experience.
But you must keep your side of the bargain. An angry
armoured bear is the most terrifying fighting-machine
known to man. I've seen one knock an Eskimo's head clean
off his shoulders with just one whack of his paw.

1ST GUEST. When was that?

GENERAL. Well, it's rather an interesting story. It was in the
Tungusk campaign, when I was in charge of a . . .

They move away. The MACAW-LADY *and the* 2ND
GUEST *are eying* LYRA.

2ND GUEST. So *she's* the child! One can see the resemblance.

MACAW-LADY. My dear, it was the *resemblance* that caused
all the trouble in the first place!

LYRA. Why they looking at us?

LORD BOREAL *can be seen across the room. A couple of*
GUESTS *observe him with interest.*

3RD GUEST. I see Lord Boreal's back in London.

4TH GUEST. Yes, he travels for half the year. And the strange
thing is, that wherever he says he's going, he never arrives.

3RD GUEST. Do you mean that he's really gone somewhere
else?

4TH GUEST. Oh, very much else, and very much further.

3RD GUEST. You mean that he travels to other . . . ?

The 4TH GUEST *puts a finger to her lips.*

4TH GUEST. Ssh! Not so loud.

LORD BOREAL *is addressing his group.*

LORD BOREAL. Oh no, Lord Asriel won't be troubling us for quite some time.

LYRA. Pan, listen!

They approach and listen.

5TH GUEST. When did they arrest him?

LORD BOREAL. I think the minute he set his foot on the Arctic snows. Click went the handcuffs, clang went the prison door, and I'm hoping they dropped the key through a hole in the ice.

All laugh maliciously.

The word from on high is that we're not to gloat. Well, I'm gloating I can tell you, I'm gloating like anything.

They move away.

PANTALAIMON. In *prison!*

LYRA. Do you think Mrs Coulter knows?

PANTALAIMON. Behind you.

MRS COULTER *is there.*

MRS COULTER. Don't look so gloomy, darling. People will talk!

LYRA *and* PANTALAIMON *find themselves near another group, which includes* PROFESSOR HOPCRAFT *and the* MACAW-LADY.

HOPCRAFT. Would you believe, Lord Asriel's photogram actually showed the Dust collecting around the human form?

6TH GUEST. Was it an adult human, Professor?

HOPCRAFT. Of course. Children have no attraction for Dust, none whatsoever. That's what the General Oblation Board was formed to investigate.

6TH GUEST. And why 'Oblation'?

HOPCRAFT. An 'oblate' is a sacrifice. The word goes back to the middle ages, when parents used to give their children to the Church to be monks or nuns.

MACAW-LADY. Or eunuchs!

HOPCRAFT. Yes indeed, in which case the sacrifice was a radical one. But as to what it might be these days, you'll have to ask our delightful hostess.

LYRA (*to* PANTALAIMON). I'm getting such a creepy feeling.

PANTALAIMON. Me too.

6TH GUEST. The children don't suffer, I hope? I wouldn't like to support anything cruel.

HOPCRAFT. Oh no, it's utterly painless. And they come to her willingly, don't forget.

LYRA. Oh no!

PANTALAIMON. Ssh!

6TH GUEST. How many helpers does Mrs Coulter have now?

HOPCRAFT. Twenty, thirty . . . there are several of them here tonight. That gangling chap, that red-faced woman . . .

MACAW-LADY. Don't get personal, please! I'm one myself.

MRS COULTER (*calls*). Into the music room, everybody!

PANTALAIMON. I don't wanna hear no more.

LYRA. I wanna get out.

The GUESTS *are moving out.* LORD BOREAL *approaches* LYRA.

LORD BOREAL. Good evening, Lyra. I'm Lord Boreal.

LYRA. Yeah, I 'eard.

LORD BOREAL. You're a very unusual child.

LYRA. Am I?

LORD BOREAL. Yes, and I think you know it. Is Mrs Coulter keeping you busy here in London?

LYRA. Not really.

LORD BOREAL. What have you learned?

LYRA. I've learned about Dust. It only likes grown-ups, doesn't it, not children?

LORD BOREAL. How interesting.

His green SNAKE-DAEMON *slithers out from the sleeve of his jacket.*

Don't be impatient, Lilith. We're leaving soon. (*To* LYRA.) What else have you learned?

LYRA. I've learned about the General Oblation Board. And . . . children and . . . sacrifices.

LORD BOREAL. I'm delighted that Mrs Coulter has taken you into her confidence. She was worried, you know, that you might be grabbed off the streets by some over-enthusiastic helper of hers. That was the reason she brought you here. But I knew it would only be a matter of time before she recruited you. A child to catch a child . . . and what a charming snippet of bait you'll be! It's surprising, isn't it, that no-one has worked it out? 'General Oblation Board'. G.O.B . . . and then . . .

LYRA. . . . the Gobblers. Yes, it's *very* surprising.

LORD BOREAL *goes.*

PANTALAIMON. Let's go!

LYRA *grabs the alethiometer and they slip out unseen.*

Oxford. Outside THE MASTER's *study.* THE MASTER *comes out, carrying a very large suitcase. He looks round nervously, puts down the suitcase and locks the door. Turning to go, to his great alarm, he sees* FRA PAVEL.

MASTER. Fra Pavel! I thought you were in Geneva.

FRA PAVEL. What are you doing?

MASTER. I'm going to Scotland. Just for the weekend.

He glances at the large suitcase.

No, the South Coast.

FRA PAVEL. Nonsense. You're running away.

MASTER. I . . .

FRA PAVEL. Do you really suppose that you can flee the consequences of your actions? Your attempt on Lord Asriel's life was an abject farce. You let the college actually pay for his expedition. You gave Lyra into the hands of Mrs Coulter . . .

MASTER. I thought it was what you wanted!

FRA PAVEL. Did she tell you that?

MASTER. No, not exactly. I was wrong. But . . .

FRA PAVEL. Lyra has escaped. The police can't find her. Mrs Coulter's team is combing the streets to no avail. Even the Tartar guards have failed to track her down.

MASTER. I know all this, and I can't for the life of me see why everyone is going to such lengths to find a perfectly ordinary child of twelve.

FRA PAVEL. Ordinary? It has escaped your attention, then, that I have watched her, visited her twice a year ever since she was a baby?

MASTER. I've never known why.

FRA PAVEL. You are familiar, of course, with the alethiometer? Indeed, your college has one, am I not correct?

MASTER. Why do you ask?

FRA PAVEL. The Church has the only other example in the Western world. I'm its official reader. And it has warned me of a prophecy, a witches' prophecy, awesome and strange but true. A child of destiny will be born. The circumstances of Lyra's birth make clear that she is the child.

MASTER. And what is her destiny?

FRA PAVEL. Lyra will either redeem the Church, will carry it on to greater glory . . . or she will destroy it. Which of the two it will be is a secret locked in a name, a mystic name which cannot be spoken even by the witches. We don't know this name. Lyra does not know she has it. Only the witches know. And now you know why she must be found. Bring me the alethiometer.

MASTER. You mean, the one that belongs to the college?

FRA PAVEL. Obviously. Mine's in Geneva. What you are waiting for? Well?

MASTER. Lyra has it. I gave it to her.

FRA PAVEL *lays a friendly hand on* THE MASTER*'s shoulder and attempts a pleasant smile.*

FRA PAVEL. Wait in your study. You will shortly receive a visit.

London. Night and fog. LYRA *and* PANTALAIMON *hide as Tartar* GUARDS *appear. Their* DAEMONS *are wolves. The* GUARDS *pass on.* PANTALAIMON *creeps out.*

LYRA. Have they gone?

PANTALAIMON. Yeah.

LYRA *comes out and holds him.*

LYRA. Don't cry, Pan. We'll find a place to sleep.

PANTALAIMON. It's all so frightening.

LYRA. Ssh.

A late-night coffee stall appears. Among the CUSTOMERS
is a MAN *in a top hat and a white silk muffler. He eyes*
LYRA *with unpleasant interest.*

A nice ham sandwich would warm us up.

PANTALAIMON. Do you think it's safe?

LYRA. It better 'ad be, 'cause I'm starving.

They approach the coffee stall.

STALLHOLDER. Yes, love?

LYRA. Cup of coffee and an 'am sandwich, please.

PANTALAIMON. Don't look round.

TOP-HATTED MAN. You're out late, my dear.

PANTALAIMON. Ignore him.

LYRA. I *am* doing.

STALLHOLDER. Here you are, me love. That'll be two
groats.

TOP-HATTED MAN. Allow me.

He pays.

LYRA. Can I have more sugar?

STALLHOLDER. Certainly, love.

The TOP-HATTED MAN *produces a brandy-flask.*

TOP-HATTED MAN. Wouldn't you rather have some brandy
in your coffee?

LYRA. No, I don't like brandy.

TOP-HATTED MAN. I'm sure you've never had brandy like
this before.

PANTALAIMON. I said, ignore him.

TOP-HATTED MAN. And where are you going to, all alone?

LYRA. I'm going to meet my father.

TOP-HATTED MAN. Oh, your father? Is he someone very important?

LYRA. Yes, he's a murderer.

TOP-HATTED MAN. A what?

LYRA. A murderer. It's his job. He's doing a murder tonight. I got his soap and towel in here, 'cause he's usually all covered in blood when he's finished. There he is now. He looks a bit angry.

The TOP-HATTED MAN *backs away, as* LYRA *and* PANTALAIMON *move away fast.*

PANTALAIMON. Lyra the liar!

LYRA. Got rid of him, though, didn' I?

PANTALAIMON. *Now* where're we going?

LYRA. Dunno. We'll have to find a derelict house or summat.

A security-light flashes on and a siren blows. Two TARTARS *appear with* WOLF-DAEMONS. LYRA *and* PANTALAI-MON *run and are nearly caught. One of the* TARTARS *collapses, shot with an arrow. The other is felled by a second arrow.* LYRA *and* PANTALAIMON *run into the arms of two gyptians,* TONY COSTA *and* BEN, *armed with bows and arrows.*

TONY. Don't scream! It's us!

LYRA. Who?

TONY. Tony. Tony Costa, Billy's brother. From Oxford, remember? This is my mate Ben, best bow-and-arrow man in the gyptian nation.

BEN. Tartar warriors, those were. Come on, let's not hang about.

They move on fast.

LYRA. What're you doin' in London, Tony?

TONY. Well, after you left, there was more kids taken than ever before . . .

BEN. . . . and us gyptians got hit a lot worse than most . . .

TONY. . . . except for the foreigner kids and the homeless
   kids . . .

BEN. Aye, they're cunning, those Gobblers.

LYRA. Tony, I know all about the Gobblers. It was them what
   sent those wolfy people after me.

TONY. Aye, well, we catched a Gobbler, didn't we, Ben . . . ?

BEN. . . . yeah, and you don't want to know what we done to
   him, but he talked all right. He said they take the kids up to
   the Arctic and they do experiments on 'em. Like cutting 'em
   up, or summat.

LYRA. *Cutting them up?*

BEN. Don't want to upset you, gal, but it's how it sounded.

TONY. So when John Faa heard what they were doin' . . .

BEN. . . . he's the Lord of the Western gyptians . . . .

TONY. . . . he said, 'Now's our chance . . . '

BEN. 'The bow is bent and the arrow is drawn an' we've a
   hazy outline of the target . . .

TONY. . . . so we'll charter a ship to sail to the Gobblers'
   Arctic hideout . . .

BEN. . . . an' we'll rescue Billy an' all the rest . . .

TONY. . . . an' bring 'em back home!'

LYRA. When are you sailing?

BEN. Now!

TONY. Tonight!

BEN. So you look after yourself, gal.

LYRA. Oh, Tony, listen . . . I saw a photogram of a man in the
   snow with his hand held up, like this . . . like he was calling
   me to the Arctic . . . and Lord Asriel's in prison there . . .
   and Roger's also there, that I swore to rescue. I gotta come
   too.

A rusty old hulk appears. On board, JOHN FAA *is about to
address six leading* GYPTIANS, *who are purposefully
sharpening knives and scythes. The aged* FARDER CORAM
is among them. LYRA *is there with* PANTALAIMON. JOHN
FAA *carries a very large hammer with him at all times.*

1ST GYPTIAN. Hold it, Lord Faa. For the hundredth time,
what's this little brat doing on board?

2ND GYPTIAN. . . . eatin' our food . . .

3RD GYPTIAN. . . . wigging 'er ears at all our secrets?

Complaints mount as:

JOHN FAA. Shut up, the lot of you! This little brat is here at
the special request of Farder Coram, who's a seer and a
spirit-talker and as wise as a tree of owls. So, Farder Coram,
if you'd *briefly* explain your reasoning, I'd be grateful.

FARDER CORAM. Thank you, Lord Faa. The roads of chance
are long and winding. Them as follows 'em oft-times lose
their way . . .

There are signs of great impatience all round.

It's all to the point, but I'll jump to the nub of it. When
I was in Oxford, Lyra, I heard that the Master give you an
object that can help us on our journey. May I see it? Look
in my eyes, and see if you trust me.

LYRA *takes out the alethiometer and shows it to him.*

It's an alethiometer all right. I seen one in China-land many
years back. Do you know how to ask it questions, Lyra?

LYRA. Sort of.

FARDER CORAM. And can you sort of read the answers?

LYRA. No, not really . . .

Groans of irritation from the GYPTIANS, *and:*

JOHN FAA. With all respect to your age and wisdom, Farder
Coram, if she can't work this thing, then it's no more use to
us than a busted alarm clock.

FARDER CORAM. I say we give her a chance. Lyra?

LYRA. Yeah, all right.

The men watch sceptically as:

I'll ask it if I'm really safe from Mrs Coulter . . . or if she'll find me.

She sets the needles.

The Madonna for her, and the baby for me, and this dragon thing, 'cause that means searching . . . well, it's one of the meanings.

She holds it in front of her like a microphone.

'Will Mrs Coulter find me?'

She looks at the dial. The GYPTIANS *yawn, stretch out and roll their eyes in boredom.*

JOHN FAA. Well?

LYRA. I'm trying!

Louder:

'Will Mrs Coulter find me? Will she . . . '

FARDER CORAM. Lyra, if you yell at it like a drunken donkey-driver, it'll tell you nothing. It's got feelings, just like we have. Sit yourself easy. Now let your mind go free . . . and when the answer comes, reach down . . . and further down, till you find the level.

LYRA *relaxes. More mutterings from the* GYPTIANS.

LYRA. It's moving! Yeah . . . The thunderbolt . . . twice at the baby . . . and a serpent an' a thing like a lizard with big pop eyes . . . and three times at the elephant. I got it! She's sending . . . a thing to find me . . . up in the air, I think . . . yes, flyin', flyin' an' spyin', nasty, angry, lock it up fast . . . and arrivin' soon. No, now. Right now. It's here.

They look round.

1ST GYPTIAN. Well I can't see it.

2ND GYPTIAN. Nor me.

3RD GYPTIAN. Still waiting.

JOHN FAA. Back to business. Lyra, go and play over there.

She moves away disconsolately. JOHN FAA *unrolls a map.*

This, friends, is where we're a-heading to. The port of
Trollesund, on the southernmost tip of the land of ice.

2ND GYPTIAN. So now we know where the Gobblers are.

3RD GYPTIAN. Aye, meeting over.

They get up.

JOHN FAA. Sit down! The Gobblers only *arrive* at Trollesund.
Then they take the kids to their laboratory, which is further
inland, we don't know where. We've got to find that out,
along of getting what else we need. Guns, on top of our
wretched knives and arrows. Some kind of fighting machine,
to match with theirs. Transport . . . What you lookin' at?

The GYPTIANS *are staring at a porthole.*

2ND GYPTIAN. What's that?

A small black object flies into view. The GYPTIANS *scatter.*
BEN *traps it in a beer glass, where it rattles around trying
to escape.*

BEN. I got it! I got it!

JOHN FAA. What in the devil's name is it?

FARDER CORAM. It's a spy-fly, John, sent snooping after us
by the Gobblers. African magic, this is. Gimme your
smoke-leaf tin.

Someone does and he manoeuvres the spy-fly into it.

It's built of clockwork that won't never run out, and pinned
to the spring, there's a bad spirit with a spell through its
heart. This thing's so monstrous angry at being cooped up,
that if it ever got out, it'd tear and rip and slash the first
creature it come across.

LYRA. What did I tell you? I can read it!

JOHN FAA. Maybe you can an' maybe you can't, but one thing's certain. If just one of these little devils warns the Gobblers we're a-coming, we'll have lost the only advantage that we got. Surprise. So we got to act fast. We got to reach their hideout, an' attack 'em before they're ready. And we don't even know where they are!

A GYPTIAN *calls from out of sight.*

GYPTIAN. Land ahoy!

Trollesund. The GYPTIANS *arrive in a desolate landscape. They look round cautiously.* PEOPLE *of Trollesund appear behind them, eyeing them shiftily and keeping their distance.*

1ST GYPTIAN. So this is Trollesund . . .

3RD GYPTIAN. Where the Gobblers brought our kids . . .

JOHN FAA. We gotta get out by nightfall. Tony and Ben, you go into town. Ask whoever will talk to you, have they seen any kids and where did the Gobblers take 'em. You men go with them. Jake and Barnaby, look around town for a rifle or two. Farder Coram, I want you to take Lyra back to the ship for safety. Don't move from there, not either of you, you hear me? The rest of you, help me look to our transportation.

All go but LYRA *and* FARDER CORAM.

FARDER CORAM. Good, he's gone. I'm off into town meself. I've got a message to send to a notable witch from around these parts. You do as he told you, gal.

He goes.

LYRA. A *witch?*

PANTALAIMON. It's what he said.

LYRA. Come on.

She and PANTALAIMON *move on.*

PANTALAIMON. What're we doing?

LYRA. We're gonna be helpful.

PANTALAIMON. What, like finding kids?

LYRA. Yeah, kids'd be good. Or clues. Or Gobblers, even.
Or . . .

She sees something.

PANTALAIMON. What?

LYRA. I can't *believe* it!

PANTALAIMON. *What?*

LYRA. You know how we en't got no fighting-machines?

PANTALAIMON. Yeah?

LYRA. Well, what's the most terrifying fighting-machine
known to man? That can 'knock off an Eskimo's head . . . '

PANTALAIMON *is as excited as she is.*

PANTALAIMON. *An armoured bear?*

LYRA. Yeah! Look.

IOREK BYRNISON *comes into view. He's breaking up a
big iron buoy.*

PANTALAIMON. He hasn't got no armour.

LYRA. He must have taken it off to work.

PANTALAIMON. He looks a wreck.

A BEAR-KEEPER *comes out with a bottle of spirits, which
he pushes fearfully towards* IOREK *with a stick.* IOREK
drinks from the bottle.

Uh-oh. He's a drunk as well.

LYRA. He's still an armoured bear, though, isn't he? Let's go
and get him.

She moves forward.

PANTALAIMON. Don't! You're mad!

LYRA *approaches* IOREK. PANTALAIMON *follows
nervously.* IOREK *glares at* LYRA.

IOREK. Who are you?

LYRA. I'm Lyra Belacqua and I got a job to offer you.

IOREK. I've got a job.

LYRA. This is a better one. An' I can pay you. I got two gold
dollars.

IOREK. I don't need gold. I need meat and spirits, and these
people pay me plenty of both.

LYRA. Yes, I can see that. You've got empty bottles all round
you. You even *smell* of drink. Haven't you got any self-
respect?

PANTALAIMON. Ssh, Lyra!

IOREK. None.

PANTALAIMON. Let's go.

LYRA. Shuddup! (*To* IOREK.) Don't you even want to know
what I want you do? It's fighting. It's fighting the people
who come to Trollesund with their stolen kids.

IOREK. I've seen those people. They're called the child-
cutters. I hate them. But I can't fight them for you.

LYRA. Why?

IOREK. Because I can't fight anyone.

LYRA. Why?

  IOREK *roars in desperation.*

IOREK. Because I've got no armour!

LYRA. There's all this metal lying around. Why don't you
make some armour out of that?

IOREK. It's useless to me. I made my armour out of iron that
fell from the skies in a trail of flame. Without it, I am
nothing. I cannot go to war, and war is the sea I swim in
and the air I breathe. My armour is my soul, just like your
daemon is your soul. And it's been taken from me. The
humans in this town gave me spirits to drink until I fell

asleep, and then they took my armour away from me. I tried
to find it, but I couldn't, so I went mad with rage. Now
I must work in this yard until I have paid for the buildings
I broke and the people I killed.

LYRA *takes out the alethiometer.*

LYRA. I've got a way of answering questions. If I can find out
where they've hidden your armour . . .

IOREK. Then I'll tear this town apart until I've got it. And I'll
fight your enemies. And I'll never drink spirits again.

LYRA. But you mustn't hurt anyone if I ask you not to. Do
you promise on your honour?

IOREK. On my honour.

LYRA. All right, I'll ask.

She sets and reads the alethiometer.

It's in the house of the priest.

IOREK *raises himself up and roars in frustration.*

IOREK. I want to get it now!

LYRA. Why don't you?

IOREK. Because I promised to work till sunset!

LYRA. If you're as small as me, it's sunset now. Look.

IOREK *crouches to her height.*

IOREK. You're right.

He roars and bounds away.

GYPTIANS *appear in the middle of a furious altercation.*
Some want revenge on the TOWNSPEOPLE*; some are furious*
with JOHN FAA *for not knowing where they have to go on to.*
FARDER CORAM *tries to interject with no success.*

BEN. This town is evil! Evil!

2ND GYPTIAN. Let's just get out!

SEVERAL. Aye! Out!

SEVERAL MORE. Aye, back to London!

1ST GYPTIAN. We asked the priest, had he seen any kids, and he set his bloody dogs on us!

He shows a rip in his trousers.

BEN. Never mind that, you 'alf-arsed idiot! Tony, show him what we found.

TONY *turns out a sack. The* GYPTIANS *gasp with horror at the sight of the contents: children's clothes and toys.* TONY *picks up a toy train.*

TONY. This is our Billy's. I made it meself!

4TH GYPTIAN. That's my Ron's jacket.

3RD GYPTIAN. This is our Daisy's.

The GYPTIANS *erupt in fury.*

4TH GYPTIAN. Let's kill all the people here!

TONY. Aye, cut their treacherous throats!

BEN. Burn down their buildings!

1ST GYPTIAN. You brung us to hell, where there en't no hope of travelling further on!

4TH GYPTIAN. 'Cause I don't believe that there *is* no further on!

2ND GYPTIAN. Aye, where're we goin'?

SEVERAL. Where're we goin? Where? Where?

The chorus grows. FARDER CORAM *somehow tops it.*

FARDER CORAM. Friends, listen to me!

They fall silent and listen.

When the present is dark and the future is yet unknown, it is the long-betided past which . . .

The GYPTIANS *groan in frustration.*

All right, I'll jump to the practical bit. There's a creature approaching that's been sent to us by a long-lost friend of my youth-time days.

He calls upwards.

Kaisa!

They all look upwards. KAISA, *a snow-goose, appears and lands.*

KAISA. Farder Coram! It's lucky you called. I wouldn't have recognised you in a month of Sundays.

The GYPTIANS *back off in alarm. A confused chorus arises:*

2ND GYPTIAN. It's a daemon!

3RD GYPTIAN. But there en't no human attached!

1ST GYPTIAN. It isn't right!

3RD GYPTIAN. Chase it away!

2ND GYPTIAN. Shoot it, somebody!

FARDER CORAM. Friends, have no fear! This kind and intelligent snow-goose, is the daemon of the Queen of the Lapland witches. For witches, you see, can send their daemons a whole sight further than what we can. Tell me, Kaisa, is Serafina Pekkala still young and beautiful?

KAISA. She is, and she remembers you as handsome as ever you were.

A knowing sigh of 'Ah's' arises from the GYPTIANS.

FARDER CORAM. What does she say?

KAISA. She thanks you for your message, and she wonders why you thought the Trollesund folk would help you, when they make all their money from the Gobblers.

FARDER CORAM. Does she know where the children are?

KAISA. Indeed she does, and I've been sent to guide you!

Cheers, and:

JOHN FAA. What kind of a place have the Gobblers taken 'em to?

KAISA. It's the worst of places. We don't know what they do there, but there's hatred and fear for miles around. Even the little lemmings and foxes keep their distance. That's why it is called 'Bolvangar'. 'Fields of evil.'

The GYPTIANS *deluge* KAISA *with questions:*

JOHN FAA. Is it strongly guarded?

BEN. How many days away?

4TH GYPTIAN. What do they do to them? What's this 'cutting'?

LYRA. Is there a boy called Roger there?

KAISA. Be silent! Who is this child?

LYRA. I'm Lyra Belacqua.

KAISA *looks at* LYRA *with great intensity.*

KAISA. Lyra Belacqua? My queen will be mightily interested to know you've come.

LYRA. Why?

KAISA. Let's say for a start, because of Lord Asriel, and his plan to travel between the worlds.

LYRA. Like to the city in the Northern Lights?

KAISA. That world is one, but there are many . . . many . . . others. They are not in our universe, but they're here, right next to us, close as a heartbeat, linked with the world we know. I spread my wings . . .

He spreads his wings.

. . . and brush ten million other worlds, and they know nothing of it. Tell me, Lyra . . .

The BEAR-KEEPER *appears, followed by the* MAYOR *and angry* TOWNSPEOPLE.

BEAR-KEEPER. That's the girl, your worship! She was whispering to the bear, and he went rampaging off!

MAYOR. Gyptians! Gyptians! Always the same!

JOHN FAA. What's goin' on?

LYRA. I found a bear, and he's gonna come with us, that's what.

The GYPTIANS *are alarmed.*

GYPTIANS. A *bear?*

JOHN FAA. Lyra, what in the name of all that's wonderful made you think we wanted a bear?

MAYOR (*to* JOHN FAA). Oh you know nothing about it, I suppose?

He continues, while the TOWNSPEOPLE *chip in with insults and the* GYPTIANS *answer with abuse.*

That bear is ours! You've got no right to him, none. It's not two weeks since he went roaring drunken around the town, tore down the bank and the police-station too, not to mention three innocent citizens lying dead as a doornail in the street!

JOHN FAA. Oh Lyra, Lyra!

LYRA. They'd stolen his armour! It's only natural that he got a bit annoyed. Please let's take him! He'll be a wonderful fighter, and he's fierce and strong . . . !

JOHN FAA. Lyra, he's as likely to kill us as he is the Gobblers.

LYRA. He's not! He won't hurt anyone if I ask him not to. He's given me his word of honour.

JOHN FAA. Honour? That's a human thing. What does a bear know about honour?

LYRA. I looked in his eyes, and I trusted him. I could *see* it, Lord Faa.

There is a loud crash of a wooden house being knocked down. The PRIEST *rushes into view.* IOREK *appears in his rusty armour. Everyone scatters.* IOREK *chases the* MAYOR *and prepares to kill him.*

LYRA. Iorek! Don't do it!

Slowly, IOREK *releases the* MAYOR.

MAYOR. Put this beast in chains!

MEN *advance with chains and nets.*

LYRA. No, don't!

A shot rings out and one of the MEN*'s hats flies off.*

MAYOR. Who did that?

LEE SCORESBY *appears with his rifle. His daemon is* HESTER, *a hare.*

HESTER. We did. Back off.

The MAYOR *and* TOWNSPEOPLE *scurry back.*

JOHN FAA. Who are you?

LEE SCORESBY. Scoresby's the name, Texan by birth, sharp-shooter by profession, temporarily stranded here with my balloon-for-hire and a cargo of rifles, owing to a certain local prospecting outfit that never paid my fee.

HESTER. Howdy, Iorek.

IOREK. Hello, Hester. Hello, Lee!

LEE *and* IOREK *embrace.*

JOHN FAA. Do you know this bear?

LEE SCORESBY. Sure do. Iorek Byrnison an' me fought in the Tungusk campaign together. He's an awkward critter, and he ain't exactly looking his best right now, but give him a wash and a brush-up, and he'll be the greatest fighter that you ever saw.

JOHN FAA. So what would you think to him joining our rescue expedition?

LEE SCORESBY. Take me too and I might consider it.

HESTER. Not so fast. What'll you pay?

JOHN FAA. One hundred dollars for the two of you plus your cargo.

HESTER (*outraged*). One hundred dollars! That's ridiculous!

LEE SCORESBY. Done.

He shakes JOHN FAA's *hand. Cheers.* JOHN FAA *addresses the* GYPTIANS.

JOHN FAA. Friends! We're fit and set and ready to go. Kaisa the goose-daemon will be our guide to the Gobblers' hide-out. Iorek the bear will be our fighting-machine. And Mr. Scoresby the balloonist will be our bank of rifles and our key to the skies. Now we can strike the Gobblers hard and fearful. We'll leave 'em ruined and waste and torn in a thousand pieces and scattered to the four winds.

GYPTIANS. Aye!

JOHN FAA *raises his hammer.*

JOHN FAA. My hammer is thirsty for blood. She can smell it in the wind from the North. She spoke to me last night and told me about her thirst, and I said 'Soon, gal, soon! Your time is coming!'

GYPTIANS. Aye! Blood! To the rescue! To Bolvangar!

They set off. IOREK *takes* LYRA *on his back and pounds alongside.*

The Northern snows. Dusk. It's cold. KAISA *flies ahead. The expedition follows. They slow down.*

JOHN FAA. Halt! We're close enough. Here's where we'll stop for the night.

GYPTIANS *point upwards and call.*

GYPTIANS. Look out! Spy-fly!

A spy-fly buzzes into view.

KAISA (*calls*). Have no fear! I'll head it off, and meet you all at our destination. Farewell!

The GYPTIANS *settle down to sleep for the night.* JOHN FAA *approaches* LYRA *and* PANTALAIMON.

JOHN FAA. I been thinking, Lyra, that your symbol-reader thingummy could be useful. First thing in the morning, ask it how many Gobbler-soldiers there are. I'll come and help you.

He goes.

LYRA. *Help* me! What a cheek.

PANTALAIMON. Ask it now.

LYRA *consults the alethiometer.*

LYRA. It's strange. It's saying that there's a Gobbler place quite near, with Tartar warriors. And they're guarding something . . . it's like a child, but it isn't a child.

PANTALAIMON. Maybe it's Roger.

LYRA. Let's go and look, when they're all asleep.

IOREK *appears.*

What's that?

IOREK. Farder Coram asked me to put his smoke-leaf tin into something stronger.

He gives it to her.

Keep it for him.

LYRA. It's beautiful.

IOREK. We armoured bears can do anything with metal. A delicate watch or a railway engine, it's all the same. What is inside it?

LYRA. One of them angry spirits.

She puts it to her ear.

Very angry. Mrs Coulter sent it after me.

IOREK *reacts with horror and amazement.*

IOREK. Do you know her?

LYRA. Mrs Coulter? Yes, she's my worst enemy! What has she got to do with you?

IOREK. She destroyed me! If it wasn't for her, I would still be the heir to the throne of Svalbard, home of the armoured bears.

LYRA. What did she do to you?

IOREK. I had a rival, Iofur Raknison, a bear of enormous strength, but vain and scheming. Mrs Coulter plotted with him against me. They bribed a bear to challenge me in single combat, and I . . .

LYRA. Couldn't you beat him?

IOREK. Oh, I did. But our code of honour is strict. Once I had won the fight, I should have spared his life. But Mrs Coulter had inflamed him with a poison, so that he kept on fighting. I was forced to kill him. That was a terrible crime. I was cast out of Svalbard to wander the Arctic like a vagrant, till I came to Trollesund.

LYRA. Yeah, she's bad enough for all of that.

IOREK. There's more. Iofur Raknison seized the throne of Svalbard. He pulled down our ancient fortress of ice and built a palace of stone and marble. Then Mrs Coulter promised to get him a daemon, as though he were a human being! Once that thought was planted in his crafty brain, he could never be free of it. Now he dreams of daemons, talks of daemons, longs for a daemon. Worst of all . . .

LYRA. What?

IOREK. . . . . she did all this, not from some foolish desire to improve our lives. She just wanted gaolers.

LYRA. *Gaolers?*

IOREK. She wanted the strongest, stubbornest creatures, in the farthest fortress of the earth, to keep her prisoner where he

couldn't escape. And there he will stay, till his heart stops
beating.

LYRA. Is he . . . Lord Asriel?

IOREK *stares at her in amazement at this double
coincidence.*

IOREK. Do you know Lord Asriel *too?*

LYRA. Yes, he's my uncle! Iorek, listen! Once we've rescued
Roger, and all the kids, we'll go to Svalbard. We'll free
Lord Asriel, and we'll win your throne back, and . . .

IOREK. Do you think, if that were possible, that I wouldn't
have done it already? Iofur Raknison has an army of five
hundred bears, each as mighty as me . . .

LYRA. Then we'll trick him.

IOREK *laughs and shakes his head.*

IOREK. No-one can trick a bear.

LYRA. *You* were tricked by the people in Trollesund.

IOREK. I drank spirits. That's a human thing to do. If I'd been
true to my bear-like nature, they would never have got the
better of me. Bears can see deceit, we see it as plain as arms
and legs. It isn't a skill, it's nothing we've learned. It's a gift
we were born with. Just as you have a gift. You can read
your truth-telling machine, but grown-ups can't. As you are
to them, so am I to a human being.

LYRA. So when I'm a grown-up . . . will I not be able to read it?

IOREK. There is a different kind of gift. But bears don't have it.

He yawns enormously.

I must rest.

He goes. LYRA *looks at the spy-fly box, puts it away.*

LYRA. Let's look for Roger.

They creep quietly away and through the snows.

We'll rescue Roger, and then we'll go to Svalbard, and I'll
give Lord Asriel the alethiometer . . . and I'll show him how
I can read it . . . and I'll use it to set him free. And then
he'll thank me, won't he? He won't be calling me
bothersome or disgusting. And he'll . . .

PANTALAIMON. Forget it.

LYRA. Why?

PANTALAIMON. 'Cause you can't trick bears.

LYRA. You can't trick bears as long as they're true to their bear-
like nature. But Iofur Rakniwhatsit's trying to be a human
being, isn't he? So maybe he's trickable.

WOLF-DAEMONS *howl. Tartar* GUARDS *are seen
patrolling.*

PANTALAIMON. Tartars.

LYRA. Ssh.

They hide. The GUARDS *move on.* LYRA *and*
PANTALAIMON *creep out.*

PANTALAIMON. There's nothing here.

LYRA. Look.

A small FIGURE *can be seen a distance away from them,
facing away.*

Roger? Rodge, is it you?

The figure becomes clearer as it turns towards them. It's
BILLY COSTA. *He looks white, drained and half-alive and
speaks in a feeble whisper.*

BILLY. You seen my Ratter?

LYRA. That en't Rodge. It's Billy Costa. Billy, what's wrong?

PANTALAIMON, *very alarmed, approaches* BILLY *and
searches all around him.*

PANTALAIMON. *He's got no daemon!*

BILLY. I lost my Ratter.

PANTALAIMON. That's what the Gobblers are doin' to 'em,
Lyra. They're cuttin' their daemons off!

LYRA. Oh Billy!

BILLY. Ratter? Ratter?

He collapses. Tartar GUARDS *re-appear with their*
WOLVES. *They capture* LYRA *and carry her to . . .*

*. . . Bolvangar. Searchlights, a high fence, a watchtower.
Tartar* GUARDS *manhandle* LYRA *off the sledge. A* NURSE
appears. She has a spooky, robotic manner of speech.

NURSE. Welcome to Bolvangar. What is your name?

PANTALAIMON (*quietly*). Don't tell 'er.

LYRA. It's Lizzie. Lizzie Brooks.

NURSE. Hello Lizzie. Have you come a long way? Those
clothes will need a wash. Let's get you changed.

She starts putting LYRA *into an institutional gown.*

We'll put your shoulder-bag in your very own locker.
What's inside it? Let's see.

She discovers the spy-fly box and the alethiometer.

Oh dear. What a funny old box. And what's this? A
compass? We'll get you something pretty and soft to play
with, like a doll or a nice woolly bear.

LYRA. I want them back. And I'm keeping the bag as well.

NURSE. All right.

She hands them back.

You have arrived in time for supper. The girls are already
eating. You can talk to them, but not to the boys. Tomorrow,
you and your daemon will be weighed and measured. Come
along.

She leads LYRA *to the canteen.*

PANTALAIMON. I'm too frightened to look. Have they all got daemons?

LYRA. Yeah, don't worry.

She joins a queue at a food-hatch. They collect food and eat after saying grace: 'For what we are about to eat, we thank the Authority.' Meanwhile:

Hello.

DARK-HAIRED GIRL. Hello.

LYRA. I'm Lizzie.

DARK-HAIRED GIRL. Hello, Lizzie.

LYRA. What's going on?

DARK-HAIRED GIRL. Nothing much.

PLUMP GIRL. It's just boring really. They give us tests, and then they lie us down and they take our temperature.

LYRA. Yeah, it sounds pretty boring.

PLUMP GIRL. They're always going on about our daemons. Finding out how heavy they are an' all. They got a weighing-machine, and your daemon gets onto it, and then they write things down and take his photo.

DARK-HAIRED GIRL. But it's the Dust they're measuring.

PLUMP GIRL. Yeah, they talk about Dust non-stop.

RED-HAIRED GIRL. I en't dusty. I had a shower yesterday.

PLUMP GIRL. It isn't that kind of dust. It's Special Dust. Every grown-up gets it in the end. That's what *she* says.

RED-HAIRED GIRL. The pretty lady.

DARK-HAIRED GIRL. Mrs Coulter.

LYRA. Is she here now?

RED-HAIRED GIRL She *wasn't*, but she's coming today to look at a new machine.

PLUMP GIRL. Here's the boys.

RED-HAIRED GIRL. We're not supposed to talk to 'em, but some of us manage!

They laugh. A NURSE *appears.*

NURSE. Remember girls! No talking, smiling or passing notes!

A NURSE *doles out pills, which they all swallow. A group of* BOYS *comes in and they queue for food.* ROGER *is among them. He and* LYRA *see each other and make secret contact. The* BOYS *go to their table and eat.*

ROGER. I can't *believe* it! How did you *get* here?

LYRA. I was kidnapped. Are you all right?

ROGER. No, I never been so frightened ever.

LYRA. Why does the nurse talk in that funny way?

ROGER. They're all like that. They're like machines or summing. And their daemons are 'arf-dead too. It weren't so bad when Billy was here. Then last week they Read 'Is Name Out.

LYRA. What'ya mean?

ROGER. They Read Your Name Out, and you gotta go with 'em. There's one boy says that they give you an operation, an' he heard what a nurse was saying. She said to a kid, we're not going to kill your daemon or nothing, it's only a cut. But I en't seen Billy anywhere, not since then. Get away, she's back.

LYRA *moves away. The* NURSE *addresses the* CHILDREN.

NURSE. Children, listen carefully. In a few moments we will have a fire-drill. It's for you to practise getting dressed and making your way outside without any panic. When the bell rings, you must stop whatever you're doing, and do what the nearest grown-up tells you. That's what you must do if there's a real fire.

The fire-alarm goes.

That is the fire-alarm. Go outside and collect your warm clothes as you go.

LYRA *and* ROGER *go out with the other* CHILDREN *and peel off.*

LYRA. Walk faster.

ROGER. Where we goin'?

LYRA. Where they can't see us.

They reach a building with a large red sign on the door: ENTRY STRICTLY FORBIDDEN.

Now listen. There's a whole load of gyptians coming to rescue us any minute.

ROGER. Honest?

LYRA. Yeah! And it en't just gyptians neither. There's an armoured bear, an' a man who flies a balloon from Texas an' a witch's daemon, only there en't no witch.

ROGER *is very upset.*

ROGER. Oh Lyra! What an 'orrible trick to play!

He continues as KAISA *appears and lands.*

You come all this way, an' then all you can do is make up stories! Lyra the liar!

He sees KAISA.

KAISA. Greetings, Lyra.

ROGER. It's true!

LYRA. I told you. Greetings to you, Kaisa. Where's the gyptians?

KAISA. There's been a small delay.

LYRA. Oh no!

KAISA. It seems the spy-fly had reported their position. The better news is that Serafina Pekkala and her band of witches are coming as well. May I suggest that this young gentleman prepares the children for a rapid escape?

ROGER. That me?

PANTALAIMON. Tell them we're gonna set off the fire-alarm . . .

KAISA. That's very good thinking, Pantalaimon.

LYRA. . . . yeah, an' then they all gotta run outside . . . and take their anoraks and their boots and stuff or they'll freeze to death. Go on.

ROGER goes.

KAISA. You must hide. Mrs Coulter's coming over the brow of the hill in a dog-sleigh.

LYRA sees the forbidden door.

LYRA. I'll go in there.

PANTALAIMON whimpers.

PANTALAIMON. No!

KAISA. What's the matter, Pantalaimon?

PANTALAIMON. I have a very unpleasant reaction to that door.

VOICES (*from offstage*). She went this way. / Yes, here are her footprints!

LYRA. I gotta go somewhere!

She opens the door. It swings open, revealing a cage filled with severed DAEMONS, pressing their faces to the wire and crying. PANTALAIMON leaps into LYRA's arms.

KAISA. Where are the children of these daemons?

LYRA. They've been cut away. That's what they do here.

PANTALAIMON. Save them! Save them!

KAISA. There is no saving to be done. But I can comfort their bereavement. Go!

LYRA *runs into the arms of two* DOCTORS.

DR WEST. This is the girl!

DR CADE *sees the open daemon-cage.*

DR CADE. What's going on?

DR WEST (*to* LYRA). What have you seen? What have you seen?

LYRA. Leave me alone!

DR CADE. We can't let her go back to the other children. She'll blurt it all out, and we'll have total panic all round.

DR WEST. There's only one thing we *can* do, it seems to me.

DR CADE. What, now?

DR WEST. Why not?

DR CADE. But Mrs Coulter hasn't arrived. I thought she had to be there for each experiment.

DR WEST. That's what she *says* . . . but there's no scientific justfication for it. She simply enjoys watching.

DR CADE. Then we just won't tell her. The shock will certainly prevent the girl from talking. Where's Dr Sargent?

DR WEST. In the laboratory.

They enter a laboratory. DR SARGENT *is there. There's a machine with two cages – one larger than the other – and a guillotine-blade raised above it.*

DR SARGENT. Gentlemen, what very good timing. May we position the subject?

LYRA *is thrown into one cage.*

It's just this moment that I've brought the apparatus up to the testing stage. And now the daemon, please.

PANTALAIMON *is thrown into the other cage. The parting is agonising for them.*

LYRA (*cries out*). You can't touch him! You can't touch him!

DR SARGENT *attends to the machine.*

DR SARGENT. It's this new alloy in the blade that makes the difference . . . quite incredibly sharp . . . Have you the reading, Dr West?

DR WEST. I do.

DR SARGENT. Dr Cade, will you reverse the daemon-bond?

DR CADE. Coming up now.

The bond between LYRA *and* PANTALAIMON *is revealed beneath the guillotine-blade.*

PANTALAIMON. Lyra! Lyra!

LYRA. Pan!

DR SARGENT (*to* LYRA). Keep still for a moment for me, if you would. That's perfect.

The blade has risen and is about to fall. MRS COULTER *appears.*

MRS COULTER. Lyra! Stop! Let that child out this instant!

They do.

No experiments may take place when I am not in attendance. I must see each one. Each one! Now go!

The DOCTORS *go.* MRS COULTER *embraces* LYRA, *who is crying.*

Oh Lyra, Lyra. Poor, poor child. It's all right now. Don't cry.

LYRA. Oh Pan!

She embraces PANTALAIMON.

MRS COULTER. What trouble you've caused. I was beside myself. I've never been so upset. I searched for you all through London.

LYRA. You sent the Tartars after me, and the spy-flies too.

MRS COULTER. I had to, darling. Once I knew you were with those ruffian gyptians . . . and a fine job they made of looking after you. Just think what would have happened if I had arrived a moment later.

LYRA. Why do you do it? How can you be so cruel?

MRS COULTER. Lyra, Lyra, it may *seem* cruel. But it's for scientific progress . . . . and the betterment of humanity . . . and yes, for the child's own good. Just one little cut, and then it's safe from Dust for ever after.

LYRA. What's wrong with Dust?

MRS COULTER. Why, everything's wrong, my dearest. Dust is evil and wicked. It doesn't collect around sweet and innocent children . . . but just a little bit later, at what we call the age of puberty? When your daemon settles? Then Dust clusters around you, radiates to and from you . . . and the child begins to have all sorts of nasty thoughts and feelings. And all it takes to stop them happening, is a snip. A tiny snip. The daemon isn't killed. It's simply not connected. It's like a sweet little pet.

LYRA. If cutting's so good, then why did you stop them doing it to me? You should have been glad!

MRS COULTER. Darling, these are grown-up thoughts.

LYRA. They're not! There isn't a kid in the whole world that wouldn't ask you exactly the same thing. 'Cause you'd have done it to Roger, and he's my friend. And you did it to Billy Costa, and I saw him, he's no more'n a ghost!

MRS COULTER. But Lyra, you aren't Billy or Roger. You're . . . you're . . .

LYRA. What?

MRS COULTER. What did they tell you at Jordan College, about where you came from?

LYRA. Came from?

MRS COULTER. I'm asking about your mother and father.

LYRA. They said they was killed in an airship accident.

MRS COULTER. *Were* killed. Except they weren't. Your father
was . . . and is . . . a remarkable man. He . . .

LYRA. You mean he's alive?

MRS COULTER. He is. He's . . . Well, I suppose you have to
find out some day. He's Lord Asriel.

LYRA. What?

MRS COULTER. You didn't know?

LYRA. No! Lord Asriel? He's my dad? That's *incredible*. And
he survived the airship accident? Yeah, he would. He's ever
so clever. But . . . You put him in prison!

MRS COULTER. Lyra . . . !

LYRA. You put my father into a stinky dungeon!

MRS COULTER. I had no choice. Let me finish my story
before you condemn and reject me.

LYRA. Well?

MRS COULTER. The airship accident never happened. It was
just a story that Lord Asriel invented to deny the facts of the
matter. He loved your mother and she loved him. It was a
wonderful love. But she was married already. And when
you were born, her husband guessed the truth, and Lord
Asriel fought him and killed him. No-one ever denied that
the fight was a fair one, not even at the trial.

LYRA. The *trial?*

MRS COULTER. There was a trial for murder. And the end
of it was that Lord Asriel had to give up his estates, his
palaces, his enormous wealth . . . and your mother, of
course, was so distressed that she wasn't able to look after
you. So she cut herself off, she had to. And that's when
Lord Asriel did something dreadfully wrong and cruel.
He put you into the care of Jordan College, and he told the
Master that your mother should never be allowed to have

anything to do with you. She was banned and shunned from being with her very own daughter. And that's how things stayed until she came to Jordan College and spoke to the Master . . .

LYRA. You mean that . . . ?

MRS COULTER. Yes.

LYRA. You can't be.

MRS COULTER. I am. I'm your mother. Do you understand now why I put your father in prison? It was my only chance to be with you, to hug you and love you, to talk to you frankly as woman to woman. But you're exhausted, poor child. I'll put you to bed.

> THE GOLDEN MONKEY *indicates* LYRA*'s shoulder-bag.*

Oh yes. There's just one tiny thing that I have to ask you. The Master confessed . . . before his tragic accident . . . that he gave you a certain toy.

> LYRA *freezes.*

It's called an 'alethiometer'. Shall I look after it for you? Will you give it to me?

> PANTALAIMON *takes out the spy-fly tin and gives it to* LYRA, *who hands it to* MRS COULTER.

Oh, you're keeping it safe in here? It's a beautiful tin. I hardly like to cut into it.

> *She finds a knife on the operating table.* THE GOLDEN MONKEY *watches closely as she cuts.*

I'm longing to see what it looks like. Here we are.

> *With a furious buzz, the spy-fly shoots out and crashes into the* MONKEY*'s face.* MRS COULTER *is injured by proxy. Crashes and explosions are heard.* LYRA *presses the fire-alarm. It rings and the din is heard of excited* CHILDREN *congregating.* LYRA *and* PANTALAIMON *run out into smoke, bullets and shells. Snow is falling.* ROGER *rushes into view.*

ROGER. Lyra! Come on! The kids are waiting!

CHILDREN are seen waving excitedly to approaching GYPTIANS, who arrive and rescue them. Tartar GUARDS attack. DOCTORS and NURSES attack. LEE SCORESBY fights back, sharpshooter style. IOREK lays Tartar GUARDS flat. MRS COULTER appears with her GOLDEN MONKEY. Both are wounded in the same place. ROGER points to the skies.

ROGER. Look! There's women flying on branches!

WITCHES appear, led by SERAFINA PEKKALA.

SERAFINA. Lyra Belacqua!

LYRA. Who are you?

SERAFINA. I'm Serafina Pekkala! Seize my hand! We're flying to Svalbard!

LYRA grabs SERAFINA with one hand and ROGER with the other. Fire and explosions. MRS COULTER extends her arms upwards, cursing in frustration.

End of Act One.

ACT TWO

Oxford / Oxford. The Botanic Gardens. Night. WILL *and* LYRA *as before.*

WILL. So . . . while you were ballooning over the icebergs, I was standing . . . trying very hard not to be noticed . . . at a bus shelter here in Oxford. It was midnight and I'd killed a man. I'd actually killed him. Me. I'd heard the thwack of his head as it hit the floor. And I'd run, I'd pelted down the stairs and legged it into the night. With this. This green leather case that started it all.

LYRA. What I understand much better now, is how many different forces were moving us on.

WILL. I knew the cops'd be after me. By the morning there wouldn't be a single police car buzzing past that didn't have my name and photo.

LYRA. There was what I wanted. And there was what you wanted. And there was what the grown-ups wanted, which was mostly completely different. But there was also . . . something bigger than all of us put together . . .

WILL. I didn't know what they did to twelve-year-old murderers, but it wouldn't be nice . . .

LYRA. . . . like an enormous wind, sweeping us forwards . . .

WILL. . . . and while I was standing . . . shaking with fear . . . I saw a cat on the pavement. A tabby. It had one paw up, and it was patting at something.

LYRA. . . . giving us chances and challenges . . .

WILL. It was a window in the air. We saw so many of 'em after that, but this first time is the one I remember best. I looked, and there was Cittàgazze.

LYRA. . . . taking us to places we didn't even know existed.

WILL. There were little waterside shops and cafés and the smell of the sea and a warm wind . . .

LYRA. Our fate.

WILL. . . . and palm trees.

LYRA. Our destiny.

WILL. So I went through.

In the basket of LEE SCORESBY*'s balloon.* SERAFINA PEKKALA, *on her branch of cloud-pine, tows the balloon, which is encrusted with frost and icicles.* LYRA, IOREK *and* ROGER *are asleep in the basket.*

SERAFINA. Are the children asleep?

LEE SCORESBY. They certainly are, and Iorek too. They won't wake up till we get there.

SERAFINA. It won't be long now. See that black line ahead of us? That's the Svalbard cliffs. We'll have to keep our height as we fly over them, or the cliff-ghasts will be swooping up after us all, and me in particular. They've a great liking for witch-flesh.

LEE SCORESBY. Can't you make yourself invisible?

SERAFINA. I can empty my head of thought so that a short-lived mortal won't *notice* me. That's not invisible, quite, and it wouldn't prevail against the cliff-ghasts. They have no human sensitivities for me to cancel out, just hates and appetites. And what will you do, Mr. Scoresby, once we get there?

LEE SCORESBY. I'll set down the kids, since that's what the little gal's determined on. And Iorek too, though I think he's crazy. I told that critter a thousand times, one bear against five hundred isn't a war. It's plain suicide.

SERAFINA. But Iorek has sworn to stay with Lyra until he dies, and that he will do.

LEE SCORESBY. She's pretty important, yeah?

SERAFINA. Are you sure she's asleep?

LEE *checks.*

LEE SCORESBY. Sure is.

SERAFINA. Then I can tell you that she's more important than
you can imagine. We witches fly where the veils between
the worlds are thin. We hear the whispers of the immortal
beings who pass from one to the other. And it's from those
whispers that we've knitted ourselves a prophecy. It's
in our poems, our spells, the bedtime songs that we sing to
our children. It tells of a child whose name can never be
spoken. A child that we know is Lyra. A child who has it in
her power to bring about the annihilation of death and the
triumph of Dust.

LEE SCORESBY. Are you saying that Dust is real?

SERAFINA. I know it's real.

She shows him her amber spyglass.

There was a traveller from a different world who gave me
this, my amber spyglass. See for yourself.

She hands him the spyglass. He looks through it.

LEE SCORESBY. I can't believe this. What am I looking at?

SERAFINA. It's Dust, Mr. Scoresby. Breathing and thinking
and flowing to where it will. That is what makes our world
a living place. And that's why we witches must keep Lyra
safe and sound until the prophecy's run its course.

LEE SCORESBY. So the future's fixed? She's like some
clockwork doll, that you wind up and set on a path that
can't be changed? Where's her free will?

SERAFINA. We are all subject to the fates. But we must act as
though we are not, or die of despair. And Lyra, most of all,
must think her fate is malleable. If she tries to follow the
prophecy blindly, she will fail. But if she acts in ignorance,
out of her own true impulse, then she . . .

PANTALAIMON *appears.*

LEE SCORESBY. She's awake.

LYRA *appears.*

Hi kid.

LYRA. I was fast asleep. Aren't you freezing, Serafina Pekkala?

SERAFINA. It's chilly enough. But then I think of what I'd be missing if I wrapped up warm. The tingle of the stars . . . the music of the Aurora . . . and the silky touch of the moonlight on my skin. Don't try it yourself, you'd die in seconds.

The balloon lurches.

LYRA. What's happening?

SERAFINA. We're flying off-course.

LEE SCORESBY. Hell, we're way too high. I'm gonna release the pressure.

He pulls on a rope. Gas escapes from the balloon and it starts rapidly dropping. ROGER *and* IOREK *wake.*

ROGER. Help! Help! We're falling!

LEE SCORESBY. Nobody panic! I just gotta pull on this.

ROGER. I'm gonna be sick!

LEE *pulls on another rope to control the descent.*

LEE SCORESBY. That ought to stop it.

LYRA. We're still falling!

SERAFINA. Look out for cliff-ghasts!

LEE SCORESBY. Aw heck, the rope's frozen up. Give us a hammer.

LYRA *helps him pull at the rope.* ROGER *looks for a hammer.*

IOREK. Stand aside! I'll do it.

He goes to the rope. The basket lurches.

ROGER. Please, please! Somebody stop us!

IOREK pulls at the rope and it comes off. He falls backwards and the basket lurches. A CLIFF-GHAST *climbs over the edge of the basket.* LYRA *and* ROGER *scream.*

IOREK. It's only a cliff-ghast.

He cuffs it and it disappears.

ROGER. Look, there's another!

Another appears. IOREK *lunges at it. The basket rocks.*

LYRA. Iorek, stay where you are! We're tipping over!

She lurches over the edge.

ROGER. She's falling out!

LYRA *and* PANTALAIMON *fall out into the snow.* SERAFINA *and* IOREK *call from above.*

SERAFINA. Lyra! I'll come back and find you!

IOREK. Stay away from the fortress! Wait for me!

ROGER. Lyra! Lyra!

They are carried off and out of sight. On the ground, LYRA *sits up, stunned.*

LYRA. Pan? Where are you?

PANTALAIMON. In your pocket.

He appears out of her pocket as a mouse.

Are you hurt?

LYRA. Dunno. Is there any more of those ghastly thingummies?

PANTALAIMON. Yes, there!

Two CLIFF-GHASTS *appear.* LYRA *and* PANTALAIMON *cower as they approach.* BEARS *appear out of the darkness and attack the* CLIFF-GHASTS, *who flee. The* BEARS *circle around* LYRA *and sniff her with suspicion. Then:*

CHIEF BEAR. Did you fall out of the balloon?

LYRA (*terrified*). Yeah.

CHIEF BEAR. Was Iorek Byrnison with you?

About to deny it, LYRA *remembers that no-one can trick a bear.*

LYRA. Yeah.

CHIEF BEAR. Come wi' us.

They walk on.

STUPID BEAR. Where are we taking her, Sarge?

CHIEF BEAR. To see the king, of course, in his marble palace.

DISGRUNTLED BEAR. 'Marble Palace!'

CHIEF BEAR. Now, now, it isn't for us to scoff. That palace were Mrs Coulter's doing, to make us all more civilised-like.

DISGRUNTLED BEAR. 'More civilised-like!'

LYRA. Is she there now? This Mrs Coulter person?

CHIEF BEAR. No, she's not. She's off on her travels, meeting popes and presidents.

DISGRUNTLED BEAR. 'Popes and presidents!'

STUPID BEAR. Mrs Coulter's going to make it so that we all get daemons, isn't she, Sarge?

CHIEF BEAR. That's what she tells us, so we gotta believe it.

DISGRUNTLED BEAR. Oh, it'll happen all right, you mark my words. Along with all the rest of her fancy notions. Reading and writing and making us cook our food. What I wouldn't give for a mouthful of raw walrus.

The BEARS *slaver with desire at the thought of raw walrus.*

CHIEF BEAR. No grumbling, if you please!

They have arrived at IOFUR RAKNISON's *palace. Other* BEARS *are assembled there. To them:*

> Greetings, brothers! Find his majesty, and humbly inform him that we've brought the prisoner.

> BEARS *go out to take the news.*

LYRA. Have you got other prisoners here at Svalbard? Or is it just me?

CHIEF BEAR (*to* LYRA). Do you see that window?

> *He points to a brightly-lit window very high up.*

> That is Lord Asriel's prison.

> *He moves away.* LYRA *looks up at the window.*

LYRA. It's like a star at the top of the sky. So bright an' far away. An' you just can't get to it.

> PANTALAIMON *pops up out of her pocket.*

> Pan, I've got an idea.

> *An army of* BEARS *appears.* IOFUR RAKNISON *enters.*

BEARS. Hail, King Iofur Raknison!

IOFUR. Bring forth the prisoner.

> *A* BEAR *brings* LYRA *forward.*

> You may kneel.

> *She does.*

> Are you a spy?

LYRA. No! No I'm not!

IOFUR. Then what were you doing with Iorek Byrnison? Don't deny it! You were in the balloon beside him!

LYRA. I'm his daemon.

IOFUR. His *daemon?*

LYRA. Yes.

IOFUR. Clear the court!

The other BEARS *withdraw.*

If you're deceiving me, you will be fed to the starving wolves.

LYRA. I know but I'm not.

IOFUR. How did that renegade outcast get a daemon?

LYRA. It was an experiment at Bolvangar. There was a doctor pressed a button, and I appeared.

IOFUR. Liar! No daemon has ever appeared in human form!

LYRA. It's 'cause . . . I'm an animal's daemon. Humans have animals, and animals have humans. It's like, back to front, all right?

IOFUR. And how can you travel so far away from Iorek Byrnison?

LYRA. I'm like a witch's daemon. And beside . . . he's not very far away. He's coming to Svalbard really soon, and he's gonna raise up all the bears against you . . . 'cause he's heard how they grumble about you.

IOFUR *roars.*

Wait, wait, wait . . . And I don't want that to happen, I don't, 'cause he's a poor, sad, drunken disgrace of a bear, and you're a king with a magnificent palace. So what you gotta do . . . you gotta tell your guards, that when he arrives . . . they mustn't attack him . . .

IOFUR. Not attack him?

LYRA. . . . . an' I'll pretend that I'm still on his side . . . and then you gotta challenge him in single combat! On your own! And when you've beaten him, that'll prove that you're the strongest, and then I'll belong to you! I'll be your daemon! I'll have a little throne of my own, right next to yours, and humans will come from all over the world to wonder at you! Iofur Raknison, the bear with a daemon!

IOFUR. You're lying.

LYRA. I'll prove it. Ask me a question. Something only a daemon would know the answer to.

IOFUR. Tell me what creature it was that I first killed.

LYRA. I'll do it. Shut your eyes and count to ten.

He does. LYRA *reads the alethiometer.*

Oh, poor thing. No wonder he turned out bad.

IOFUR *opens his eyes.*

IOFUR. Well?

LYRA. You were brought up by your mother, all alone. And when you were young, you were hunting on the ice, and you got into a fight with an older bear from a different tribe. You killed him, and you took his head back home for your mother to see, and she knew who he was. He was your father.

IOFUR *is greatly moved.*

IOFUR. How did you know my secret?

LYRA. I'm a daemon.

BEARS *approach excitedly.*

BEARS. Iorek Byrnison is here! / Shall we kill him? / We'll tear him to pieces.

IOFUR. Leave him to me. I'll kill him in single combat. Bring my armour!

BEARS *(call).* Let him approach! / Spare his life! / The king has commanded!'

They dress IOFUR *in armour.* IOREK *appears in his rusty armour and collapses in exhaustion.* LYRA *runs to him.*

LYRA. Oh Iorek, I've done a terrible thing. You've got to fight Iofur Raknison all alone, and you're hungry and tired . . .

IOREK. How did this happen?

LYRA. I tricked him! Oh, I'm sorry.

IOREK. You are no longer Lyra Belacqua. Your name for ever after will be Lyra Silvertongue.

LYRA. You mean I haven't done wrong?

IOREK. Done wrong? To fight him is all I want!

IOFUR addresses the crowd.

IOFUR. Bears! Hear my command! If I kill Iorek Byrnison, his flesh will be torn apart and scattered to the cliff-ghasts. His head will be stuck on a pole above my palace gates. His name will be blotted from memory. Iorek Byrnison, I challenge you!

IOREK addresses the crowd.

IOREK. Bears! If I kill Iofur Raknison, I'll be your rightful king. My first order to you, will be to tear down this palace, this perfumed house of mockery and tinsel, and hurl it into the sea. Iofur Raknison has polluted Svalbard. I shall cleanse it.

IOFUR and IOREK square up for the fight. They prowl round, sizing each other up. They pause, then leap together with a crash. They fight and IOREK's left forepaw seems to be wounded. IOFUR taunts him.

IOFUR. Broken-hand! Whimpering cub! Prepare to die!

IOREK leaps at him: the injury was only a feint. He tears off part of IOFUR's jaw. IOFUR shrieks. IOREK sinks his teeth in his throat. IOFUR dies.

IOREK. Behold! I eat the heart of the usurper!

He tears out IOFUR's heart and eats it.

Now who is your king?

BEARS. Iorek Byrnison!

They rush to support IOREK, whose strength is near giving out. ROGER appears.

ROGER. What happened? Have I missed it?

LYRA. Iorek ate the other bear's heart.

ROGER. Eurgh! Yuk!

LYRA. Come on, we're going to find Lord Asriel.

She pulls him along through the palace and up stairs.

ROGER. The balloon crashed into a mountain. And then that goose arrived and said that one of the witches got made a prisoner at Bolvangar, so Serafina went back to rescue her. She was frightened the witch might tell them something. Then . . .

THOROLD *appears.*

THOROLD. Lyra! Little Lyra! Come in, child, and bring your friend with you. The Master is in his study.

He shows LYRA *and* ROGER *through a door.*

LYRA (*to* THOROLD). What's a study doing in a prison?

THOROLD. You know the Master. He hadn't been here a month before he'd twisted the bears around his little finger. They gave him books and instruments and a laboratory too. He was both prisoner and prince.

LYRA *goes into the library.* LORD ASRIEL *sees her.*

LORD ASRIEL. Lyra! Get out! I did not send for you!

LYRA *is dumbfounded.*

LYRA. What?

ROGER *comes in.*

STELMARIA. She's brought a friend.

LORD ASRIEL. Who's this boy?

LYRA. He's Roger. You saw him at Jordan College.

LORD ASRIEL *looks hard at* ROGER. *Smiles.*

LORD ASRIEL. I'm delighted to see you, Roger. Thorold, run these children a hot bath.

THOROLD. Follow me.

He leads ROGER *out.* LYRA *stays. After a moment:*

LORD ASRIEL. Why haven't you gone?

LYRA. I'm not a bloody kid, to be put in a bath when you feel like it. You're my father, en't you?

LORD ASRIEL. Yes. So what?

LYRA. So what? You should have told me before, that's what. You could've asked me to keep it secret, and I would've. I'd have been so proud that nothing would have torn it out of me. But you never.

LORD ASRIEL. How did you find out?

LYRA. My mother told me.

LORD ASRIEL. Your mother . . . ? Then there's nothing left to say. I don't intend to apologise, and I refuse to be preached at by a sanctimonious ten-year-old.

LYRA. I'm twelve! I'm twelve!

LORD ASRIEL. Well, you would know. And if you want to stay, you'd better make yourself interesting to me. What did you see on your way here? What have you done?

LYRA. I set you free, that's what I done. You can go.

LORD ASRIEL. I'll go when I'm ready. What else?

LYRA. I brought you this. The Master give it me.

She shows him the alethiometer.

I hid it and I treasured it and I kept on going, even with Tartars and Gobblers catching me, and being nearly cut away from Pantalaimon. And after all that, when I walked in the door, you looked horrified, like I was the last thing in the world you wanted to see.

LORD ASRIEL. But Lyra . . . you were.

LYRA. Right, that's it. You're not my father. Fathers love their daughters. But you don't love me, and I love a moth-eaten old bear more than I love you. Here, take it anyway.

She puts down the alethiometer where he can reach it.

LORD ASRIEL. I can't read that thing. It will only annoy me. Keep it.

LYRA *is about to tell him that she can read it.*

LYRA. But . . .

LORD ASRIEL. Don't argue!

He gives it back to her. She's very upset.

LYRA. So it was all for nothing.

LORD ASRIEL. Nothing? What would you say if I told you that you'd helped me? That in your childish innocence, you'd brought me the key to a door that had never been opened? And that behind that door, lay the greatest adventure that the human race has ever known?

LYRA. I dunno what you're talkin' about.

LORD ASRIEL. Well, think. You were at Jordan College. You overheard my lecture. Didn't you understand what I was saying?

LYRA. Yeah, 'course I did! There was Dust, and the man with his hand held up like that. An' it was him what gave you the amber something? Wasn't it?

LORD ASRIEL. He gave me that and a great deal more.

LYRA. There was the palm trees, and the Roarer . . .

He laughs.

LORD ASRIEL. The Roarer!

LYRA. Don't laugh! I gotta find out these things. What's a . . . nylation?

LORD ASRIEL. A nylation?

LYRA. Yeah. A nylation of death. What's the Triumph of Dust? What if you're just a clockwork doll, but nobody tells you? What's Dust anyway?

LORD ASRIEL. Either you've been eavesdropping more than I suspected, or you've an uncanny imagination. Dust is what makes the alethiometer work. You can look at it, you can test it. It thinks. It settles on what is grown and made and changed. It's the physical proof that something happens when innocence becomes experience.

LYRA. Like how?

LORD ASRIEL. Like Adam and Eve in the Garden of Eden. Do you know what original sin is?

LYRA. Sort of.

LORD ASRIEL. Eve fell, and Dust flooded into the world. That's why the Church detests it. They hate to see their power being challenged by something so wise and beautiful and vivid. Your mother made use of that. She wanted power and, being a woman, she couldn't achieve it the normal way. So she approached a particularly nasty branch of the Church . . . the Consistorial Court of Discipline . . . and proposed a scheme to suppress this hideous, sinful, poisonous substance. They were delighted. They gave her money, influence, spies, permission to kill, all in the name of their supreme commander, the Authority.

LYRA. Is it only her what does the cutting? You've got machines and stuff. What about you?

LORD ASRIEL. Cutting in itself is of no interest to me. It's just random cruelty. My experiment draws on something that your mother's bumbling doctors never noticed. When the daemon-bond is severed . . . cut right through . . . it releases an burst of energy. Greater than any earthquake, any bomb ever made. If we could *use* that energy . . .

Pause.

LYRA. We could travel to other worlds.

He smiles approvingly.

LORD ASRIEL. Good, you're learning.

LYRA. There's millions of other worlds, en't there?

LORD ASRIEL. There are as many worlds as there are possibilities. I toss a coin. It comes down heads. But in another world, it comes down tails. Every time that a choice is

made, or a chance is missed, or a fork in a road is taken . . .
a world is born for each of the other things that *might* have
happened. And, in those worlds, they do. Somewhere out
there, in one of those worlds, is the origin of all the death,
the sin, the misery, the destructiveness in the world. That's
original sin. And I'm going to destroy it. Death is going to
die. There is a weapon . . .

LYRA. You never said nothing about any of this. Not at Jordan.

LORD ASRIEL. Do you really imagine that I'd tell those
scholars what I was really planning? If the Church
suspected, for one moment . . .

STELMARIA. You've told her enough.

LORD ASRIEL. Stelmaria is right. Have your bath.

LYRA. Can we talk in the morning? Will you tell me more?

LORD ASRIEL. Of course. You're my daughter, aren't you?
Now go.

He turns away from her. LYRA goes.

Bolvangar, partly destroyed. SERAFINA *is alone. She makes
herself invisible.* MRS COULTER *appears with* DR SARGENT.
They don't see her.

MRS COULTER. We have a visit from the Church? But why?
They could hardly have come at a worse time.

DR SARGENT. I assume it's just a run-of-the-mill inspection.

MRS COULTER. Dr Sargent, you are most naïve. I hardly
think Fra Pavel and a party of senior clerics have flown all
the way from Geneva for any such humdrum reason. What
did they say to you?

DR SARGENT. They asked about Lyra . . .

MRS COULTER. Lyra . . . ?

DR SARGENT. . . . and the witch you captured.

A scream is heard from inside a building.

They've taken her for interrogation.

MRS COULTER. They had no right. That witch is *mine*! I took her in battle.

She goes into a damaged building. Inside are FRA PAVEL *and other* CHURCH BUREAUCRATS. *A* WITCH *is bound to a chair. She has been tortured.*

YOUNG CLERIC. Why won't she tell us?

BLUNT CLERIC. Witches don't feel pain in the way that humans do.

YOUNG CLERIC. Do you think it's possible that we've been interrogating the wrong person?

BLUNT CLERIC. You mean we ought to ask Mrs Coulter?

MRS COULTER *comes in.*

MRS COULTER. Ask me whatever you like. Go on. Or would you rather tie me up and torture me, like you've done to the witch? A witch who happens to be the private property of the General Oblation Board!

SERAFINA *is there with a knife. Nobody sees her.*

FRA PAVEL. There is no General Oblation Board. It's been closed down and its records have been expunged. Your spy-flies are decommissioned, and your bank account in Geneva was terminated at midnight.

MRS COULTER. I can explain what happened.

FRA PAVEL. We know what happened. The Church's entire investment in Bolvangar has been wiped out. We know that your daughter was responsible. What we do not know, and are here to find out, is her precise identity.

MRS COULTER. Forgive me, Fra Pavel, this is much too subtle for me to understand. Just what are you talking about?

FRA PAVEL. What do you know about the witches' prophecy?

MRS COULTER. I've never heard of it. What does it say?

FRA PAVEL. It states that Lyra is either the Church's greatest friend or its darkest foe.

MRS COULTER. Lyra? My daughter? Why did none of you tell me? How long have you known?

FRA PAVEL. Since she was born. We stood over her at her cradle, we have followed her ever since and we'll continue thus until we have discovered which of the two she's going to be.

MRS COULTER. Well, I'll do all that I can to help.

FRA PAVEL. I thought you might. Where is she now?

MRS COULTER. She's flown to Svalbard.

FRA PAVEL. Correct.

MRS COULTER. May I go?

FRA PAVEL. No. The key to her destiny lies in a name, a secret name, that only the witches know. This stubborn creature here refuses to tell us. Make her.

MRS COULTER. Now?

FRA PAVEL. Yes, now.

> MRS COULTER *takes the* WITCH*'s hand.*

MRS COULTER. Well, witch! You heard Fra Pavel. What is the name?

> *The* WITCH *shakes her head.* MRS COULTER *breaks one of her fingers.*

> *Now* will you tell us?

WITCH. Never!

FRA PAVEL. Try again.

MRS COULTER (*to the* WITCH). What is the secret name? Tell us, or I will break *all* your fingers!

> *The* WITCH *cries.*

WITCH. It is the name of one who came before. You always feared her! And now she has come again!

YOUNG CLERIC. Lyra's our enemy!

MRS COULTER. That's not what she said!

BLUNT CLERIC. We must arm the zeppelin and fly to Svalbard.

FRA PAVEL (*to* MRS COULTER). Continue.

MRS COULTER. Must I?

FRA PAVEL. We need the name.

MRS COULTER *turns slowly to the* WITCH.

MRS COULTER. Well?

She breaks another finger.

WITCH. Let me die!

SERAFINA PEKKALA *becomes visible.*

SERAFINA. I am here.

WITCH. Serafina Pekkala! Take me!

SERAFINA PEKKALA *stabs the* WITCH.

FRA PAVEL. Seize her!

SERAFINA *draws her bow and arrow. Pandemonium.* SERAFINA *escapes.*

The Palace at Svalbard. Night. The BEARS *are celebrating.* THOROLD *weaves his way through the crowd.*

THOROLD. Miss Lyra! Miss Lyra!

LYRA. What's up?

THOROLD. The master's packed a sledge and gone up North.

LYRA. He can't! He said we'd . . .

THOROLD. And he's taken the boy. Your Roger. Don't you remember? He said 'I did not send for *you*.'

LYRA. You mean he'd sent for someone else?

THOROLD. He'd sent for a child to finish his experiment. That's his way. Whatever he wants, he calls, and along it comes.

LYRA. And I walked in . . . and he thought it was me. But he's not gonna do what I *think* he is? He *can't*.

PANTALAIMON. He will! He'll do it for *sure*. He wants that burst of energy.

LYRA (*calls*). Iorek!

IOREK. Bears! March on to the mountains! Now!

LYRA *rides on* IOREK BYRNISON'*s back. Other* BEARS *follow.* PANTALAIMON *flies above them.*

LYRA (*to* IOREK). Faster! Fast as you can!

IOREK. What's that sound?

LYRA. There's a zeppelin coming after us!

An amplified voice is heard from the zeppelin: 'Lyra Belacqua! We can see you!'

PANTALAIMON. Whose is it?

LYRA. It's the Church! The Church!

Machine-gun fire is heard.

IOREK. Bears! Go faster! Let's get ahead of them!

They march on, then stop at a snow-bridge.

IOREK. Stop! This bridge is made of snow. It will not carry my weight.

LYRA. I'll go on my own. And if ever we meet again . . .

IOREK. . . . I'll fight for you as though we'd never been parted. Goodbye, Lyra Silvertongue.

LYRA. Goodbye, King Iorek Byrnison.

She dismounts. He goes. To PANTALAIMON:

Let's go.

She crosses the bridge. It threatens to collapse.
PANTALAIMON *flies above.*

PANTALAIMON. Look! The Aurora!

They've reached a mountain-top. LORD ASRIEL *is there
beside a sledge/laboratory, which is like a home-made version
of the Bolvangar cutting-machine.* ROGER *is there, tied up.*
SALCILIA, *his daemon, is in a cage.* LORD ASRIEL *is
uncoiling a wire and giving the end of it to a bird which flies
upward and out of sight.*

ROGER. Lyra! He's got my daemon!

LYRA. Father!

LORD ASRIEL. Lyra! Get away! This is nothing to do with
you.

LYRA. Don't touch his daemon! Leave her alone!

LORD ASRIEL. If you distract me now, I swear I'll strike you
dead.

PANTALAIMON *runs to release* SALCILIA. LYRA
releases ROGER.

LYRA. He's my friend! Don't you care about that!

ROGER. Lyra, help!

LORD ASRIEL (*to* LYRA). Stay where you are! Stelmaria!

PANTALAIMON *carries* SALCILIA *to* ROGER.

ROGER. I've got her! I've got her!

PANTALAIMON *flies to* LYRA. LYRA, PANTALAIMON,
ROGER *and* SALCILIA *are momentarily all together.*

LYRA. Roger! Run!

STELMARIA *retrieves* SALCILIA *and gives her to*
LORD ASRIEL, *then keeps* ROGER *at a distance. The*

wire-connection shoots sparks. The Aurora dips and flares.
The guillotine in LORD ASRIEL'*s machine falls,*
separating ROGER *from* SALCILIA. ROGER *collapses.*

Roger! Roger, speak to me!

ROGER. Feel funny.

He dies.

LYRA. He's *killed* him!

MRS COULTER *is heard approaching.*

MRS COULTER. Lyra! Lyra!

PANTALAIMON. She's here.

On LORD ASRIEL'*s level, a city appears in the Aurora.*

LORD ASRIEL. Look, Stelmaria! Look!

THE GOLDEN MONKEY *bounds into view.* MRS
COULTER *follows.*

MRS COULTER. Asriel!

LORD ASRIEL. Look at that pathway! Look at the sun . . .
it's the light of another world! Don't turn your back on it,
Marisa.

She approaches him.

MRS COULTER. Was Lyra here? Did you cut her? Tell me!

LORD ASRIEL. I cut the boy. And it worked! Look at the
Dust that's bathing us both in glory. Feel the wind . . . let it
blow on your hair, your skin . . .

Their DAEMONS *move together erotically.* LORD ASRIEL
and MRS COULTER *kiss.*

MRS COULTER. Let me go!

LORD ASRIEL. I'll tell you a secret. Nobody knows but you.
I'll go through to that world, then into another, on and on,
until I've found the Authority. Then I'll destroy him.

MRS COULTER. You're insane.

LORD ASRIEL. I can do it. There's a weapon, a knife.
'Æsahættr'. It will be brought to me in a different world.
We'll use it together. We'll smash the universe into pieces,
and put it together in a new way. Isn't that what you want?
To be part of my plan?

MRS COULTER. I can't. I have to stay in this world and find
our daughter. She's in danger. She's an enemy of the
Church.

LORD ASRIEL. And you'll protect her?

He laughs.

You of all people? You lied to her. You tried to corrupt her.
You put her father in prison. If I were her, I'd run from you
as fast as my legs would take me, and I'd keep on running.

*The zeppelin is heard: 'Lyra Belacqua! Give yourself up!
Walk into an open space and raise your hands.'*

MRS COULTER. *Now* do you believe me?

LORD ASRIEL. How can she be the Church's enemy?

MRS COULTER. What have you done to deserve to know?

She starts to go.

Go to your Dust, your filth.

LORD ASRIEL. Go to your dreary, sad little machinations.
I don't need you.

He and his STELMARIA *walk into the Aurora.*

MRS COULTER (*calls*). Lyra? Lyra, were you here?

She turns and walks away and out of sight.

LYRA. What do we do? We can't go back.

PANTALAIMON. We gotta go forward, then. To where the
Dust is.

LYRA. I'm frightened, Pan.

PANTALAIMON. Me too. But if your mother, and all those
other wicked people, think that Dust is bad, it's probably
good. And don't you remember what Lord Asriel said?

LYRA. It's 'heads in one world, tails in another . . . ?'

PANTALAIMON. Roger's dead in this world . . . but there
could be another world where he's still alive. And we
promised to find him.

LYRA. Let's go.

She and PANTALAIMON *climb up, walk into the Aurora
and go through it.*

The desolate wastes of Lapland. SERAFINA *is addressing an
assembly of* WITCHES. *They include* PIPISTRELLE,
CAITLIN, GRIMHILD *and* GRENDELLA. LEE SCORESBY
is there. The meeting is in uproar.

SERAFINA. Sisters, listen to me! The prophecy has begun,
and the child is amongst us. And now the Church is after
her . . . !

PIPISTRELLE (*and* OTHERS). Do they know her name?

SERAFINA. No! Not yet! That's still our secret.

CAITLIN (*and* OTHERS). Where is she?

SERAFINA. Sisters, this is what I'm trying to tell you! She's
lost! She's lost in the maze of the worlds, and Mr. Scoresby
is here to help us find her . . .

PIPISTRELLE. We don't need any help from a short-lived
mortal . . . !

GRIMHILD. . . . that won't be walking this earth any longer
than a tadpole!

Wild chorus of agreement.

LEE SCORESBY. Ladies! I'm just a simple aëronaut, who's
hoping to end his days in comfort . . .

Boos.

. . . buy a little farm, a few head of cattle . . .

GRENDELLA. Yes, it's nice to plan for an easy life, when
we've been driven from every pleasant quarter of the earth!

More agreement.

Let's hang him upside-down from his own balloon!

Pandemonium.

RUTA SKADI. Let me speak!

SERAFINA. Ruta Skadi, Queen of the Latvian clan, I'll yield
to you and to nobody else. Let's hear you.

RUTA SKADI. Serafina Pekkala, to hear you talk, anyone
would think that destiny was a poor weak thing that couldn't
manage without our help. You're wrong. It's bigger than us.
It knows what it's doing. If the child of the prophecy has
gone wandering through the worlds, then there's a reason
for that, and every mile we fly going after her is a mile in
the wrong direction. There's a war approaching! Lord
Asriel's gone to kill the Authority. There'll be blood and
swords and thunder in heaven like's never been heard since
the proudest of all the angels was cast down into blackness.
We're *in* this war already, hate it or love it, and I say, let's
love it, let's relish and joy in the bloodshed, and it makes no
difference what strange allies we find for ourselves, as long
as we know our enemy. That's the Church. As long as it's
been on this earth, it's suppressed and persecuted everything
good about human nature. When it can't suppress it, it cuts
it out. They cut the souls out of the children at Bolvangar.
They cut out the sexual organs of boys and girls. They burn
witches! Yes, sisters! Witches like us!

A chorus of disgust and anger.

All to ravage the joy of life, in the name of that monster,
that tyrant, the Authority. If the Church is on one side, then
we witches have got to be on the other. So let's join together
to fight for Lord Asriel. And let Lyra look after herself!

Shouts of agreement and dissent:

GRENDELLA. Their war is none of our business!

PIPISTRELLE. Let the short-life mortals fight their own war!

CAITLIN. They can tear each other apart of their own accord,
just like they've always done! But we must fight . . .

A hubbub of agreement and dissent, and:

SERAFINA. Sisters, will you *listen*? We can all of us find a
reason to stand apart from human affairs, after all they've
done to us. And Ruta Skadi, your battle will come in its
own good time. But if we don't first make the prophecy
come true, then there won't be a world for you to fight in.
Lord Asriel didn't just build a pathway. He cracked the
shell of the sky. Look through my amber spyglass. What
do you see?

She passes the amber spyglass to GRENDELLA, *who looks
through it.*

GRENDELLA. Dust is flowing away . . .

There's a general gasp of worry and alarm. GRENDELLA
passes on the amber spyglass and more WITCHES *look
through it.*

SERAFINA. All through the North, raggedy doors and
windows have opened that were never there before. Dust
is falling through them into a void, an absence, and so it
will go on, worse and worse, till nothing is left, not a
breath, not a gasp, unless the child of the prophecy, true to
her secret name, brings not the defeat of Dust, not the loss
of the loveliest gift of the stars, but its joyful return. And
now you're silent. You're agreed. We must find her and
lead her towards her destiny. Do you swear to that?

A chorus of agreement.

There's one last thing. We need a guide to take us into the
world she's fled to, and there's only one man alive with the
knowledge to do so. He knows the secrets of the worlds.
He gave me the amber spyglass . . . and Mr. Scoresby will
bring us to meet him . . .

RITA SKADI *leaps up in fury.*

RUTA SKADI. You mean Jopari!

SERAFINA. Yes, Jopari!

RUTA SKADI. You deceived me! I'll kill him! I'll send him
crashing down to earth!

Howls of protest and support.

SERAFINA. Too late. You've sworn.

RUTA SKADI *fumes for a moment.*

RUTA SKADI. Then I'll come with you. Don't let me near him, though. Don't let me see him. Keep him away!

Cittàgazze. LYRA *and* PANTALAIMON *come on. They have been walking for days.*

LYRA (*calls*). Hello!

No answer.

There's nobody here either.

PANTALAIMON *bounds off towards a café.*

Hey, where're you goin'?

PANTALAIMON. There's a sandwich.

LYRA *looks at it.*

LYRA. It's days old.

She eats a bit of salami out of the middle.

There's one good thing. We're probably safe from my mother and father.

PANTALAIMON. The two most treacherous, lyingest people on all the earth.

LYRA. Wasn't it awful when they kissed like that?

PANTALAIMON. We made some friends though, didn't we?

LYRA. Yeah . . . Iorek . . . Serafina . . .

PANTALAIMON. Kaisa . . .

LYRA. Mr. Scoresby . . .

PANTALAIMON. Hester . . .

A noise is heard in the kitchen at the back of the café, frightening them both.

LYRA. What was that?

PANTALAIMON. Let's go an' look.

LYRA. We could have imagined it.

PANTALAIMON. Yeah.

LYRA. Nah, come on.

> *They approach the source of the noise.* WILL *charges out and into* LYRA. *They tussle, then pull apart and look at each other.*

WILL. You're just a girl.

LYRA. You're just a boy. You wanna make summing of it?

WILL. No! I thought that . . . never mind. What's your name?

LYRA. Lyra Silvertongue.

WILL. I'm Will. Will Parry.

> *She looks at him in horror.*

> What you lookin' at?

LYRA. What 'appened?

WILL. What?

LYRA. Did they do it to you as well?

WILL. What you talkin' about?

LYRA. Your daemon! Where's your daemon?

WILL. My *demon?*

LYRA. Yeah. Like Pan.

WILL. I haven't got no demon. I don't *want* no demon. Are you talkin' about that cat?

PANTALAIMON. I think he really doesn't know.

WILL. It talks!

PANTALAIMON. Of course I talk. Did you think I was just a pet?

WILL. That's incredible. A talking cat? Now I've seen everything. Can I pat it?

PANTALAIMON. No!

LYRA. Nobody pats another person's daemon. Never, ever.

WILL. I was trying to be nice, that's all. Where I come from, a demon is something evil, something devilish.

LYRA. Where is it? Where you come from?

WILL. It . . . No, you wouldn't believe it.

LYRA. I might.

WILL. All right. I come from a different world.

LYRA. You too?

WILL. What do you mean, you too?

LYRA. Well . . . So do I.

WILL. Honest?

LYRA. Yeah.

WILL. So . . . how did you get here?

LYRA. Through the Aurora.

WILL. Rubbish!

LYRA. What about you, then?

WILL. I came through a window in the air. Near a bus shelter in Oxford.

LYRA. That's impossible.

WILL. Yeah, and walking through the Aurora, that's just normal, I suppose. Tell you what. I'll pretend to believe you, and you pretend to believe me, and then we won't have to row. All right?

LYRA. Look, I don't mind.

WILL. You hungry?

LYRA. Yeah, starvin'.

WILL. There's eggs in there. I'll cook an omelette.

He goes to the fridge.

LYRA. Boys can't cook.

WILL. Well this boy's had to.

LYRA. In my world, servants do the cooking.

WILL. In my world, the Coke comes in cans.

He produces a couple of cartons of Coke. Gives her one.

LYRA. It's cold.

WILL. 'Course it's cold. Haven't you ever heard of a fridge?

She fiddles with the carton, baffled as to how to open it.

Look, I'll show you.

He opens the carton. Goes to the kitchen and mixes eggs to make an omelette. Two children – ANGELICA and her younger brother PAOLO – appear.

ANGELICA. Hello.

LYRA. Hello.

WILL. What's the name of this place?

ANGELICA. Cittàgazze.

WILL. Where's all the grown-ups gone?

ANGELICA. They all screamed and ran away. It's nice for kids. We can go anywhere we like, and play on the pedal-boats.

PAOLO. There'll be more kids coming back later.

ANGELICA. We're the first.

PAOLO. Us and Tullio.

ANGELICA. Shut up.

LYRA. Who's Tullio?

ANGELICA. He's our brother, that's all.

PAOLO. He's still a grown-up, en't he? He's in the tower. He's gonna . . .

ANGELICA. Shut up, I said.

They start shouting at each other.

WILL. Hold it, hold it . . . What did the grown-ups scream and run away from?

ANGELICA. The Spectres, of course.

LYRA. The *Spectres?*

PAOLO. Yeah, they eat people up from the inside out.

ANGELICA. But they don't eat kids, and kids can't see them. And there used to be just a few. But then last week, there was a huge, big bang, and a light in the sky . . .

LYRA (*to* PANTALAIMON). That was Lord Asriel's blast of energy.

WILL. What?

LYRA. Go on!

ANGELICA. . . . an a fog came down, and when it went up again, there was Spectres everywhere, millions and millions.

LYRA. You mean they're all around us? Right this minute?

ANGELICA. You got it.

PAOLO. We're looking for ice creams. Wanna come with us?

LYRA. No, not now.

ANGELICA. Snob.

She and PAOLO *go.*

WILL. Spectres all round us.

LYRA. No wonder the grown-ups ran.

WILL. They ran all right.

LYRA. Left their papers.

WILL. Left their food.

LYRA / WILL. Left their smoke-leaf / ciggies.

They look at each other.

What?

They look at a packet of cigarettes.

Is that what you call 'em?

Pause. They look at each other and begin to believe each others' story.

LYRA. That's funny.

WILL. Yeah. So what're you doing here?

LYRA. I'm looking for someone. An' I'm running away.

WILL. Who from?

LYRA. My mother, mostly.

WILL. Fed up with you, is she?

LYRA. Worse than that, 'cause I let a spy-fly loose an' wrecked her laboratory, and I found out the Gobblers' secrets and I'm summing to do with Dust. Special Dust. Not ordinary Dust, obviously.

WILL. No, obviously.

LYRA. What about you?

WILL. I'm running away as well.

LYRA. Who from?

WILL. Some people.

PANTALAIMON. Are they bad people?

WILL. Some of 'em are. (*To* LYRA.) Look, who do I talk to? You or it?

LYRA. It's 'him'. And it makes no difference. If you talk to Pan, you're talking to me in a different way.

WILL. Like on the telephone?

LYRA. What's a telephone?

WILL. Don't you know anything?

LYRA. I do! I know lots of things, but I don't know anything about your world 'cause I've never been there! That good enough for you?

She cries.

WILL. I'm sorry.

LYRA. It en't you. It's just everything that's been happening.

WILL. I do believe you now. I mean . . . I'm starting to.

LYRA. Me too.

WILL. Let's eat.

They eat.

LYRA. Except it can't be true about the window.

WILL. Well, how do you think I got here? I saw the palm trees and the . . .

LYRA. Yes, I believe the window an' the palm trees. But it can't have been in Oxford. I oughta know. I come from Oxford. Oxford's in *my* world.

WILL. Then there's two different places with the same name.

LYRA. Are there scholars in that Oxford?

WILL. Sure are.

LYRA. Is there a Jordan College?

WILL. No, I don't think so.

LYRA. So it's the same but different. Two Oxfords. In two different worlds.

WILL. Two?

LYRA. There could be more. There could be millions. 'I spread my wings, and brush ten million other worlds, and they know nothing of it.'

WILL. Who said that?

LYRA. A witch's daemon.

WILL. Right.

LYRA. A goose.

WILL. Right, right.

LYRA. You bet it's right.

WILL. So . . . are you gonna go back? To your Dusty world?

LYRA. I can't, not ever. Are you gonna go back to your different Oxford?

WILL. Uh huh.

LYRA. What's that mean?

WILL. Means I've got to, 'cause I'm looking for someone.

LYRA. Will. You know I said I was looking for someone too? Well, him an' me was best friends, and he used to live in *my* Oxford.

WILL. So?

LYRA. Can I come with you?

WILL. Yes, if you want. Just don't come trailing around after me, that's all. You'll need some proper clothes. We'll have to borrow 'em from a shop.

LYRA. What's wrong with what I got on?

WILL. My world is dangerous for me. Really dangerous. An' if people notice us, they're gonna start wondering where we come from, and then they'll find the window and I won't have this world to come an' hide in. So you gotta fit in. And don't talk to anyone. Got that?

LYRA. Yeah.

WILL. And wash your hair. And have a bath. If you go round smelling like that, you're really gonna stand out and no mistake.

He gets up.

I cooked, so you can wash up.

LYRA. I don't wash up.

WILL. Then I won't show you the window. This place doesn't belong to us. So we gotta tidy up after ourselves. I'll find a bed upstairs. Good night.

He takes the leather writing-case and goes.

LYRA. That's the grumpiest boy I ever met.

PANTALAIMON. Find out who he is.

LYRA. I will, don't worry.

She takes out the alethiometer and studies it.

PANTALAIMON. What's it say?

LYRA. It says he's a murderer. He's on the run from the police.

PANTALAIMON. Let's go.

LYRA. No, don't. It's good, in a way. It means we can trust him. And . . . it's moving again. It's telling me something I never even asked it.

PANTALAIMON. What?

LYRA. It says I gotta stop looking for Roger. I gotta stay with Will an' . . . help him find the person he's lookin' for.

She's upset.

Geneva. A corridor in the Consistorial Court of Discipline.
MRS COULTER *is waiting.* FRA PAVEL *come in.*

FRA PAVEL. Ah, Mrs Coulter.

MRS COULTER. I've been waiting half the morning.

FRA PAVEL. The President of the Consistorial Court of Discipline does not defer to the convenience of others. He is on his way. You will find him to be a practical and outspoken man. Answer him briefly and to the point. Rise.

The PRESIDENT *comes in. He sits and so do the others.*

PRESIDENT. Mrs Coulter. I'm told you come with a request, and an offer of help. I'll hear them in that order.

MRS COULTER. Father President, this is my request. The Church is pursuing my daughter as though she were some kind of public menace, and it's still not clear that there's any reason for it to do so.

FRA PAVEL. We have the evidence!

MRS COULTER. No you don't. There's a prophecy of a sort, and there's the hysterical boast of a tortured witch. That's all. What I am asking for, is permission to find my daughter myself, and to keep her in my care. And when, or if, I discover some sinister truth about her, I'll tell you.

FRA PAVEL. The impertinence!

The PRESIDENT *raises a hand.*

PRESIDENT (*to* MRS COULTER). How can you help us?

MRS COULTER. As everyone knows, Lord Asriel has caused a mighty detonation in the North. The Church has assumed that he has some evil purpose, but you don't know what it is. Well, I was there. I watched him while he walked through the Aurora. I know why he went, and what he intends to do. And I can tell you.

PRESIDENT. Bring in the gentleman outside.

An ATTENDANT *goes out.*

FRA PAVEL. Nothing that Mrs Coulter tells us should be believed, until we've got a second opinion!

PRESIDENT. That's what I'm doing.

LORD BOREAL *is shown in. He's tense and nervous.*

Lord Boreal, come in. You've met Mrs Coulter. Do you know why I've called you here?

LORD BOREAL. Well, I can see that there's a panic. One can hardly move out there for gibbering monks.

But this attempted joke goes down badly.

I'm sorry.

PRESIDENT. Lord Boreal, you have been travelling world-to-world illegally for several years. The Church has known that, and has winked at it. It now demands the benefit of your experience. If you are less than totally frank, your punishment will be severe. Do you understand?

LORD BOREAL. I do.

PRESIDENT. Mrs Coulter tells us that Lord Asriel crossed into another world through the Aurora Borealis. Can this be true?

LORD BOREAL. He would have to have found a window.

PRESIDENT. A *window?*

MRS COULTER. It's not a window. It's a hole. He used my discovery to make it.

FRA PAVEL. Be quiet!

PRESIDENT. Did you find a window?

LORD BOREAL. I did . . . years ago, quite by chance . . . one walks through it exactly as though it were a doorway . . . it's alarming at first . . . the air on the other side is different, and there's a certain quality to the light . . . I've mainly travelled . . .

PRESIDENT. Yes?

LORD BOREAL. . . . to a world which boasts an Oxford like our own. There are some differences. No Jordan College, for example. I go there often. I have a house there, where I live for half the year, under the name of Sir Charles Latrom. It's an agreeable place. The wine is good, and I have a not-too-stressful posting with the secret services. I'm sorry, I'm chattering . . .

PRESIDENT. We commend you on your frankness. Mrs Coulter, perhaps now you'll tell us what Lord Asriel plans to do.

MRS COULTER. Can I have some assurance about my daughter?

PRESIDENT. That may follow.

MRS COULTER. He plans to find the Authority, and to kill him.

PRESIDENT. *What?*

All wait, while he collects himself.

Why did the alethiometer not warn us?

FRA PAVEL (*startled*). Are you speaking to me, Father President?

PRESIDENT. I am.

FRA PAVEL. The crisis may not be as grave as it seems. There was, as we all know, a similar attack on the Authority many thousands of years ago and it failed quite miserably. There's no reason to think that Lord Asriel . . .

MRS COULTER. He's getting a knife. A god-destroying knife. Why don't you all stop talking and listen to me!

PRESIDENT. A knife? Fra Pavel, where is this knife? Can it really kill the Authority? And how can we get to it before Lord Asriel does?

FRA PAVEL. I shall ask the alethiometer. But I'm afraid that three whole questions, where one alone can take up to a year to answer . . .

LORD BOREAL. I can answer them all.

PRESIDENT. Go ahead!

LORD BOREAL. There is a world that I pass through on my way to Oxford. Its name is Cittàgazze. There's a knife there, which I'm certain is the one that Mrs Coulter has just described. It's in a tower, a tower with . . .

PRESIDENT. Can you get it for us?

LORD BOREAL. That is a different matter. My journeys through Cittàgazze have never been free from a certain anxiety. It harbours creatures . . . smoke-like, semi-invisible . . . known as Spectres. They kill their victims in a singularly revolting manner, by sucking out their souls and leaving only a lifeless husk behind.

PRESIDENT. But people live there?

LORD BOREAL. They did till recently. But I tried to go into Cittàgazze not two days ago. The city was empty of all but children. Everyone else had fled. And there were Spectres by the thousand, thronging the streets. I have never felt such terror. I would gladly get you the knife if I could. But it would be certain death.

PRESIDENT. It will be certain death if you don't.

LORD BOREAL. In fact, a line of approach has just occurred to me. There is one person alive who knows much more than I do. He is a shaman, named Jopari, much admired among the witches. But to find him, I must first return to my other Oxford.

PRESIDENT. Do so.

MRS COULTER. Good, that's fixed. And may I take possession of my daughter?

The PRESIDENT *indicates for someone else to be shown in. Meanwhile:*

FRA PAVEL. What's the point of Mrs Coulter looking after her? She keeps losing her.

MRS COULTER. At least I find her. That's more than you've ever done!

FRA PAVEL. Father President, must I listen to these insults . . . ?

BROTHER JASPER *comes in. He is keen and clever.*

PRESIDENT. Silence. This is Brother Jasper, who has been lent to us by the Society of the Holy Spirit. He is said to have been the finest alethiometer-reader ever to have passed through Jordan College. Fra Pavel, will you give him yours?

FRA PAVEL. I beg your pardon?

PRESIDENT. Give him yours. And may the Authority preserve us from incompetent clerics.

Shattered, FRA PAVEL *gives the alethiometer to* BROTHER JASPER, *who feels it with his hands and face in an intuitive way.*

BR JASPER. This won't be difficult. Where shall I start?

PRESIDENT. Begin with Lyra. Ask it about her secret name. Lord Boreal, you know your orders. Mrs Coulter, you have done us a useful service. Guard your tongue, and if all goes well you will have your daughter. Fra Pavel, wait in your study. You will shortly receive a visit.

Cittàgazze. WILL *and* LYRA, *looking.* WILL *carries a green leather writing-case.*

LYRA. I can't see anything that even *looks* like a window.

WILL. Maybe it's gone.

LYRA. No, look.

The window appears. Traffic is heard. LYRA *looks through.*

Oh, Will! It's wonderful. Only . . . what's that noise?

WILL. It's the traffic on the Oxford ring road. Don't stand in front, or they'll see your legs.

LYRA. I don't mind if they see my legs.

WILL. But there won't be a body, will there? Just two legs with nothing on top, and that'll freak 'em out big time. Get down and look from one side.

She does.

LYRA. It's not like any bit of Oxford *I* know. Are you sure it's Oxford?

WILL. Yes! Now stick that daemon of yours in your pocket, an' duck through quickly and move away fast as you can.

LYRA *and* PANTALAIMON *go through. There's the blare of a horn and a screech of brakes.*

Watch out!

He dashes through after her.

Are you all right?

They're in WILL's *Oxford.*

LYRA. I'm fine. I wasn't expecting it all to be so busy.

WILL. This isn't busy. It's just cars, an' people having their
lunch break. Let's move on, there's someone looking.

They do.

LYRA. Maybe I better stick with you for a bit.

WILL. Well, just don't talk to anyone. Not one word. You got
that?

LYRA. Yeah, all right.

They enter a busy part of town, filled with a variety of
ORDINARY PEOPLE. LYRA *stares around in amazement.*

All these people, and not one of 'em's got a daemon!

WILL. Stop staring.

They walk on.

LYRA. What's them white dots on the pavement?

WILL. Chewing gum. Don't ask.

LYRA. Don't be frightened, Will. I can protect you.

She approaches two STRANGERS.

Excuse me. Is this the way to the centre of town?

WILL *pulls her away.*

WILL. *Never* do that again.

LYRA. What you talking about?

WILL. You were calling attention to yourself. You gotta keep
quiet and still, then people won't notice you. Look, just
believe me, Lyra, I've been doing it all my life. You're not
being serious.

LYRA. Serious? I'm the best liar there ever was. I lie and
shout and make a big show, and I sort of . . . hide behind it.

And I don't get caught, not ever. You're the one who's not being serious. You're meant to be hiding from the police, and you en't got the first idea.

WILL. Who said I'm hiding from the police?

LYRA. You are, though, aren't you? 'Cause you murdered someone.

WILL. Let's go in here where it's not so busy.

The Botanic Gardens. The tree and bench are there. LYRA *looks round.*

LYRA. Will! It's the Botanic Gardens. We got one in my Oxford too, just the same. *Exactly* the same.

WILL. Never mind that. Sit down.

LYRA *does.*

How did you know about me?

LYRA. I asked this.

She produces the alethiometer.

It's an alethiometer. I ask it whatever I want to know, and it tells me.

WILL. You were spying on me!

LYRA. I wasn't! Well, not much. 'Cause then it told me to forget everything what I was plannin' to do, and help you instead. And I hate that. It makes me really angry. But it's what it said, an' I can't say no, so who're you lookin' for? Tell me.

WILL. It's my dad. He went to the Arctic on an expedition when I was still a baby, an' he vanished. His name was John, John Parry. A soldier. And when I got older . . . these men started hanging about the house, and telephoning my mum. She said they were spooks . . . like . . . secret service people?

LYRA. What did they want?

WILL. This.

He shows her the green leather writing-case. Opens it.

It's got my dad's letters inside, that he wrote from the
Arctic. The spooks kept on hassling us to get them, an' my
mother got ill, so I took her to stay with a friend. An' that
same night, I woke up to hear two men inside the house.
Rummaging round and whispering. I hid behind a door at
the top of the stairs . . . an' one of them came up, very
slowly, an' he stopped . . . an' I ran out and crashed into
him. Hilarious really, a kid like me attacking a trained killer.
Except that Moxie, my cat, was just behind him. Here.

He gestures to the back of his knees.

And he tipped right over her and crashed down the stairs.
An' he was dead. I grabbed these letters and ran, an' that's
when I came to Oxford. 'Cause there's books here, and
libraries and newspaper offices. And I can find out all about
my dad.

He takes a letter out of the writing-case.

This is the last letter he wrote. He's up in the Arctic, and
he's found an 'anomaly'. Something peculiar. He's put the
directions down, longitude, latitude, everything. It's at a
place called Lookout Ridge, and there's a rock that's shaped
like a standing bear.

LYRA. An' what's the anom . . . the anomaly?

WILL. That's what I wanna find out.

LYRA. I'll help you, Will.

WILL. You can if you like, but I don't want you using that
machine of yours. It's like cheating.

LYRA. I won't.

WILL. Why should I trust you?

LYRA. I told you about my friend. Only I didn't tell you
everything. I thought I was saving his life, and instead
I took him to the most dangerous place he could have been.
And now he's dead. I'll never betray a friend again, I promise.

She gives him the alethiometer in its bag.

Take this. Just for today. It's the most precious thing I got. It means that I trust *you*.

He takes it.

WILL. An' you take this.

He gives her the writing-case.

I'll meet you back here.

WILL*'s Oxford.* LORD BOREAL *proceeds to the desk of a cuttings library. The* LIBRARIAN *is there to greet him. An* ASSISTANT *is busy on a computer.*

LORD BOREAL. Good morning to you.

LIBRARIAN. Good morning, Sir Charles. We haven't seen you in the library for quite some time.

LORD BOREAL. I've been away. I sent a message about some cuttings I wish to read.

ASSISTANT (*to the* LIBRARIAN). I'm looking them up right now, sir.

LORD BOREAL. Only now? I did explain that it was urgent.

LIBRARIAN (*to the* ASSISTANT). Quick as you can. (*To* LORD BOREAL.) I am so sorry about this. Shall we be seeing you at the patrons' dinner on Friday? I know we sent you an invitation.

LORD BOREAL. It must be waiting for me at Limefield House. I haven't been home yet.

ASSISTANT. Was it 'P A double-R Y', sir?

LORD BOREAL. 'Parry', that is correct. Major John Parry.

ASSISTANT. I'm afraid the files are out. They must be with the young lad in the Reading Room. He said he was doing some research for a school project.

LIBRARIAN. Well, get them off him!

LORD BOREAL. Please . . . do no such thing. I'd hate to
think that I was stunting his education.

*He goes into the cuttings-room. WILL is at a table, keeping
tight hold of the alethiometer-bag and reading cuttings. LORD
BOREAL comes in, sees WILL and studies him closely. After
a moment, he sidles up, looks over his shoulder, and reads:*

'Archeological Expedition Vanishes . . . '

WILL *pays no attention.* LORD BOREAL *reads on:*

'As signals to an Alaskan Survey Station remained
unreturned today, fears grew for the lives of a party of
British explorers . . . ' How I envy you young people. You
have such fascinating things to study these days. When
I was a boy, it was all 'amo, amas, amat' and the square
of the hypotenuse.

WILL *ignores him.*

Latrom's the name. Sir Charles, but pay no attention to the
handle. My card.

He puts down a card and looks at the cutting.

That was the Nuniatak dig, was it not? I remember it well.
There were scientists, geologists and a couple of military
advisors. But of course you'd know that.

WILL. Why?

LORD BOREAL. I . . . would have thought your teacher
would have told you. The expedition never came back, of
course. It simply vanished.

He reaches over and takes another cutting. Reads:

'Legends of the North', by Major John Parry.

He reads on:

' . . . in a dingy bar, and to the sound of the baseball on the
TV, the gold-miner told me that he'd heard of this anomaly,
though he'd never seen it himself. It was, he said, a
doorway into the spirit world.'

He repeats:

'A doorway into the spirit world.'

WILL. It's no use for my school project, though, is it? It's just superstition.

LORD BOREAL. Quite so . . . Let's try another one.

He finds another cutting.

Now what can this be?

He reads:

'Days of Anguish.' With a touching photo . . . graph of mother and child.

As he continues, WILL *gradually lets go of the alethiometer-bag.*

A tragic tale. The wife almost breaking beneath the strain. The waiting days, the lonely nights. The telephone that never rings. And with a child to bring up on her own. A child of . . . six months old?

WILL *is totally absorbed in the cutting.* LORD BOREAL *goes, taking the alethiometer-bag with him.*

Cittàgazze. In the mountains. JOPARI *is tracing a large circle with his staff. He is weak and ill, and wears a shaman's cloak.*

JOPARI (*calls upwards*). Witches! Come down to rest for a moment. You'll be safe now!

RUTA SKADI *appears.*

RUTA SKADI. Jopari. Jopari, look at me.

JOPARI. I can see you. Get into the circle.

RUTA SKADI. I won't obey you. I refuse to obey you.

JOPARI. Don't be a fool, it's for your protection. I've made a space that the Spectres can't get into.

RUTA SKADI. Did you know that I was flying in Serafina's band?

JOPARI. Of course, I saw you.

RUTA SKADI. Why didn't you speak to me?

JOPARI. Because if I had, you would have killed me. Just as you would have killed me ten years ago, if I hadn't escaped.

RUTA SKADI. You rejected me then! And now that you're dying, you still reject me! I'm a witch! I don't forgive! If you're ever again in the same world as me, I swear you will die!

JOPARI. Go!

She goes. The other WITCHES *descend to earth.*

SERAFINA. Is this the world that Lyra fled to?

JOPARI. It is. You'll be safe inside this circle for a minute or two, until the charm wears off. After that, you'll be as vulnerable to the Spectres as any short-lived mortal.

The WITCHES *look round.*

CAITLIN. We can breathe.

GRIMHILD. But the air feels different.

PIPISTRELLE. When we flew through the clouds, even the rain felt different on our faces.

JOPARI. This is where I first arrived when I left my home. I walked from snow into snow, through a blizzard so dense and blinding that it was hours before I realised what had happened. I travelled South, to a colourful city, filled with palm trees and cafés and fishing boats bobbing at the quayside. And the stench of death.

SERAFINA. Jopari, you're exhausting yourself. Don't talk.

JOPARI. Three hundred years ago, the philosophers here made a knife. They wanted to divide matter . . . to cut it smaller and smaller, till they had made a particle so minute that even the strongest lens couldn't detect it . . . and then to divide that too. It worked. It worked triumphantly. But they'd unleashed a power they couldn't control. The knife cut windows into other worlds, and the Spectres floated in.

Do you see them now, as they gather around us? Drifting, shimmering, like smoke in a mirror? But you'll be safe enough, as long as you stay in the air. Good luck to you all, as you search for your child of destiny. You will not see me again. Farewell.

SERAFINA. Farewell, and thank you.

The WITCHES *go.*

LEE SCORESBY. Let's hit the trail, Jopari. I'll take you home.

JOPARI. I'm not going home.

LEE SCORESBY. You're not? But the witches told me . . .

JOPARI. I'm sure they did, but the witches know only half the story. They think they came to me of their own free will. They're wrong. I called them to me.

LEE SCORESBY. Why?

JOPARI. Because I needed you, Mr. Scoresby. I needed you, and your power of flight, to bring me into this world, and on to a tower they call the Tower of Angels. There is a man there named Giacomo Paradisi. He's old and frail but, many years ago, he fought for the knife and won it. He is the Bearer. And it is only the Bearer who can win this war for the powers of good. He has to find Lord Asriel and put the knife at his disposal. If he fails, the Authority will never be defeated. That's what I must tell Paradisi before I die. So, Mr. Scoresby, will you help me find him? You won't be safe. The Church will be after us, that's for sure.

LEE SCORESBY. Will it be good for Lyra?

JOPARI. It will be good.

LEE SCORESBY. Then I guess I'm on.

WILL*'s Oxford.* LYRA *and* WILL *are there.*

LYRA. How *could* you? I can't do *nothing* without it. Nothing! I can't find Roger. I can't know nothing about what my mother's up to . . .

WILL. Look, I said I was sorry. He distracted me. He showed me a photo of . . .

LYRA. *What?*

WILL. I've just remembered something. I've got his address.

He takes out LORD BOREAL'*s visiting-card.*

Sir Charles Latrom, Limefield House, Headington, Oxford.

LYRA. Good. We'll wait till dark, an' then we'll burgle him.

WILL. We can't.

LYRA. Iorek Byrnison would.

WILL. Yeah, I would too, if I was a ten-foot bear. Lyra, there'll be wires and alarms and lights flashing all over the place.

LYRA. So what we gonna do?

WILL. We'll go and see him.

LORD BOREAL'*s living-room. A burly* BUTLER *shows* WILL *and* LYRA *into the room.* LORD BOREAL *is reading a newspaper.*

LORD BOREAL. Will Parry? I've been expecting you. Oh yes, I know your name. There's a very good photo of you in this morning's paper.

He reads:

'Teenage suspect on the run.' It says the public shouldn't approach you, but . . .

He and LYRA *recognise each other.*

LYRA. Lord Boreal!

LORD BOREAL. Lyra Belacqua!

She makes a dash for the door, but the BUTLER *is barring it.*

LYRA. Did my mother send you?

LORD BOREAL. Not at all. Your appearance now is utterly unexpected but most welcome. Shall we talk business?

WILL. There's nothing to talk about. You stole something that belongs to Lyra, and we want it back.

LORD BOREAL. Is it this?

He takes the alethiometer out of a cabinet.

LYRA. Give it to me!

LORD BOREAL. Not yet.

He looks at it.

I had assumed that the bag you were clutching in the reading room was the case with your father's letters inside. Instead, I discovered this curious object. It would sit very nicely in my collection of antique instruments . . . but its value for me is entirely contained in the heartbroken look on Lyra's face as I hold it in front of her. I have a bargaining chip. That's all I wanted.

WILL. Give it back to us.

LORD BOREAL. Oh no, not yet. You see, there's something else that I want much more.

LYRA. Get it yourself!

LORD BOREAL. I can't. It's in a place where only children can go. Lyra, I know you've been there. Go back, and look for a tower with stone angels carved around the doorway. In that tower, there is a knife. I must have that knife. Master Parry, you'll need to fight the Bearer to get it off him. But he's an elderly man . . . he'll be no match for a hardened murderer like yourself. Get me that knife and Lyra will get her toy back. Return without it, and I'll call the police. Now off you go.

They go.

Cittàgazze. The Torre degli Angeli. LYRA, WILL *and* PANTALAIMON *approach it. An old man –* GIACOMO PARADISI *– appears at the top of the tower. He has been beaten and tied up.*

PARADISI. You down there! Run! Run! He's taken the knife!

WILL moves to get away.

WILL. Let's go.

LYRA. What you doin'? You gotta stay an' fight.

WILL. You serious?

LYRA. 'Course I'm serious! It was you that lost the
alethiometer, so you gotta get it back.

WILL. But he's got the knife an' I've got nothing.

*A young man rushes out of the door. This is TULLIO. He
has the knife in his hand. He sees WILL and stops.*

LYRA (*to WILL*). If you don't, I will!

She runs at TULLIO.

TULLIO. Get away! I'll kill you!

*WILL pulls LYRA away and turns to face TULLIO. They
fight. At first, WILL fares badly. Then he starts to fight dirty
and with determination, and wins. He and TULLIO pull
apart. WILL has the knife. TULLIO looks around in terror.*

TULLIO. Give it back! Please! You don't need it! You're just
a kid!

*LYRA and WILL watch as TULLIO sees something
terrifying approaching him. He waves his arms in the air, as
though fending off a cloud of bats. Then, unexpectedly, he
slows down and concentrates on the pattern of bricks or
stones in the tower wall. WILL is watching as though
hypnotised.*

LYRA. Come on!

*She drags WILL into the tower, and they climb the stairs
unseen. TULLIO slows down, stops and stands frozen and
immobile. LYRA and WILL appear on the roof of the tower.
GIACOMO PARADISI is there. They untie him.*

WILL. Was that the Bearer?

PARADISI. No, I am the Bearer. He stole the knife from me and, like a fool, he thought that he could use it. Only the Bearer can use it.

WILL *passes it to him.*

LYRA. Will! Your fingers! He cut off your fingers!

WILL *looks at his hand. His little finger and the one next to it are missing, and the wound is bleeding furiously.* PARADISI *sees this.*

PARADISI. You've won the knife. When I was a boy, I fought and won it, just like you. You see?

He shows his hand, from which two fingers have been severed in the same way as WILL*'s.*

These missing fingers are the badge of the Bearer. Now it has passed to you.

WILL. Look, the only reason I got mixed up in this is because of a man who wants the knife for himself.

PARADISI. I know the man you mean. Don't give him the knife. He will betray you. Take it.

WILL. No, I . . .

PARADISI. With this knife, you will be able to cut windows between the worlds. I'll show you.

WILL *takes the knife.*

Hold it ahead of you.

WILL *does.*

Now feel. You're looking for a gap so small you'd never see it, but the tip will find it, if you put your mind there.

WILL. I'm feeling sick.

PARADISI. Relax. Don't force it. The knife is subtle. Place your mind where the edge is sharpest. *Be* the tip of the knife.

WILL. I can feel . . . a snag.

PARADISI. Now think of nothing else. If for a single moment your thoughts should waver, the knife will break. Tease the point into the heart of the snag . . . and cut.

WILL cuts. A window opens. Traffic is heard.

LYRA. It's Oxford.

PARADISI. Now you must learn to close the window. That's my last lesson. Then I shall wait on this rooftop, out of the Spectres' range, until I die.

He shows WILL, using his fingertips.

Feel for the edge, just as you felt with the knife. Put your whole soul into the tips of your fingers. Then . . . pinch it.

WILL tries. LYRA and PARADISI watch. The traffic noise continues.

WILL. I can't. Just can't.

LYRA. You're trying to shut out the pain. You gotta accept it.

WILL pinches the window closed. The traffic noise stops.

PARADISI. Now you are the Bearer. You can slice the air and heal it. You can travel between the worlds. You can prevail against men, monsters, spirits, Spectres, even the most high angels. And in the war that is to come, you may be called to aim it even higher.

*

Outside the tower, SERAFINA, RUTA SKADI and other WITCHES appear.

SERAFINA. See in the sky . . . a throng of tiny lights, as fast and purposeful as a fleet of swans. Give me my amber spyglass.

She looks through it.

Ah . . . they're angels . . . Angels flying to the North Pole, just as they did those aeons ago when they made war on the Authority and were defeated.

RUTA SKADI. There was no Lyra then, and no Lord Asriel.

SERAFINA. You think it's possible, then, that they could win this time?

RUTA SKADI. I feel their victory in my witch's heart. Oh, let me join them, sister! Let me fly with the angels!

*

LORD ASRIEL *appears in his fortress.*

LORD ASRIEL.
   'Into this wild abyss, the wary fiend
   Stood on the brink of hell and looked a while
   Pondering his journey . . . '

*

MRS. COULTER *appears.*

MRS. COULTER. Lyra? Where are you?

*

WILL *and* LYRA *are with* PARADISI *on the Torre degli Angeli.*

WILL. Dad! I'm coming to find you!

*

The PRESIDENT *appears.* BROTHER JASPER *approaches him.*

BR JASPER. Father President . . . ?

PRESIDENT. Well?

BR JASPER. I have discovered Lyra Belacqua's secret name.

End of Part One.

PART TWO

CHARACTERS IN PART TWO

Between the Worlds

LORD ASRIEL *and* STELMARIA
MRS COULTER *and* THE GOLDEN MONKEY
LYRA BELACQUA *and* PANTALAIMON
WILL *and* KIRJAVA
LORD BOREAL
JOPARI

THE CHURCH
THE PRESIDENT
BROTHER JASPER
DR SARGENT

WITCHES
SERAFINA PEKKALA *and* KAISA
RUTA SKADI
GRIMHILD
PIPISTRELLE
CAITLIN
GRENDELLA

GALLIVESPIANS
LORD ROKE
THE CHEVALIER TIALYS
THE LADY SALMAKIA

BEARS
IOREK BYRNISON

ANGELS
BALTHAMOS
BARUCH

Cittàgazze

ANGELICA
PAOLO
GIACOMO PARADISI

The Land of the Dead

MR. PERKINS, *an official*
JEPTHA *and* HANNAH JONES
OLD MOTHER JONES
MOTHER JONES'S DEATH
LYRA'S DEATH
THE BOATMAN
NO-NAME, *a harpy*
ROGER PARSLOW

WITCHES, CLERICS, BEARS, GHOSTS, TARTAR GUARDS,
SOLDIERS, HARPIES *and others*

ACT ONE

Opening montage.

LYRA *and* PANTALAIMON *are running.*

LYRA. Run, Pan! Run!

*

LORD ASRIEL *and* MRS COULTER *are there.*

LORD ASRIEL. Look at that pathway! Look at the sun . . .
it's the light of another world! Don't turn your back on it,
Marisa. Feel the wind . . . let it blow on your hair, your
skin. Come with me. We'll smash the universe into pieces,
and put it together in a new way. Isn't that what you want?
To be part of my plan?

MRS COULTER *pulls away from him.*

MRS COULTER. I can't.

*

ROGER *is dying.*

ROGER. Feel funny.

LYRA *embraces him.*

LYRA. Roger! Rodge!

*

SERAFINA *addresses the* WITCHES.

SERAFINA. Sisters, listen to me! The prophecy has begun, and
the child is amongst us. And now the Church is after her . . . !

WITCHES. Do they know her name?

SERAFINA. Not yet! That's still our secret. And now we must
find her and keep her from harm until her destiny's run its
course.

*

LYRA *meets* WILL.

LYRA. Where is it? Where you come from?

WILL. No, you wouldn't believe it.

LYRA. I might.

WILL. All right. I come from a different world.

LYRA. Well . . . So do I.

*

MRS COULTER *is putting her case to the* PRESIDENT.

MRS COULTER. Father President, the Church is pursuing my daughter as though she were some kind of public menace, and it's still not clear that there's any reason for it to do so. What I am asking for, is permission to find my daughter myself, and to keep her in my care.

PRESIDENT. You'll have your daughter.

*

WILL *and* LYRA *are together.*

WILL. I'm looking for my dad. He went to the Arctic on an expedition when I was still a baby, an' he vanished. His name was John, John Parry.

*

JOPARI *appears with* LEE SCORESBY.

JOPARI. And it is only he, the Bearer of the knife, who can win this war. He has to find Lord Asriel and put the knife at his disposal. If he fails, the Authority will never be defeated. That's what I must tell him.

LEE SCORESBY. Will it be good for Lyra?

JOPARI. It will be good.

*

LYRA *watches as* WILL *and* TULLIO *fight.* WILL *wins.*

LYRA. Will! Your hand!

*

RUTA SKADI *confronts* JOPARI.

RUTA SKADI. You rejected me then! And now that you're
dying, you still reject me! I'm a witch! I don't forgive! If
you're ever again in the same world as me, I swear you will
die!

JOPARI. Go!

*

BROTHER JASPER *approaches the* PRESIDENT.

BR JASPER. Father President . . .

PRESIDENT. Well?

BR JASPER. I have discovered Lyra Belacqua's secret name.

He hands the PRESIDENT *a document. The* PRESIDENT
reads it.

PRESIDENT. Summon the Council!

Bells toll. Church DIGNITARIES *assemble in the Grand
Chamber of the Consistorial Court of Discipline, all in a great
panic.* NUN-STENOGRAPHERS *organise seating and
prepare to take notes. All kneel and make the sacred sign of the
Authority. All rise.*

PRESIDENT. The world is facing two great crises. To begin
with the one you know of: war is inevitable. Lord Asriel is
building a fortress. He is developing weapons of new and
awesome potential. Rebel angels are flocking to him in their
thousands. He plans to attack the Authority in his citadel,
the Clouded Mountain, and to destroy him.

An AGED CLERIC *wishes to speak.*

Yes, your Grace?

AGED CLERIC. Since the Authority is all-seeing and all-
powerful, won't he be better apprised than we of Lord
Asriel's plan? And won't he attack Lord Asriel first?

PRESIDENT. I don't know. I don't have direct contact with the Authority. Nobody has, not since the days of Pope John Calvin. Now if we . . .

An even MORE AGED CLERIC *wishes to speak. Impatient:*

Yes, your Eminence?

MORE AGED CLERIC. There is, I believe, a danger you've not yet mentioned? I am referring to Æsahættr, the subtle knife, the god-destroyer.

PRESIDENT. Your Eminence is correct. The subtle knife is the only weapon in the universe against which the Authority has no defence. Getting this knife, or neutralising it, is one of our major aims. We have dispatched an agent to procure this knife . . .

NUN. The agent is here, Father President.

PRESIDENT. He's here? We'll deal with this right away. Send him in.

LORD BOREAL *comes in, carrying a little box. He's just arrived, and is very nervous.*

LORD BOREAL. It is an honour to stand before you in the Consistorial Court of Discipline, and I hope . . .

PRESIDENT. Lord Boreal, have you the knife?

LORD BOREAL *mops his forehead with his handkerchief.*

LORD BOREAL. Not quite . . . but I've found a boy, who has promised to bring it to me.

PRESIDENT. When?

LORD BOREAL. Tonight.

PRESIDENT. Can you trust this boy?

LORD BOREAL. Oh absolutely . . . you see, I have in my possession the alethiometer.

He takes it out of its box.

It is my bait, my bribe . . . It's what he must fight for. I must confess I'm rather proud of this little stratagem of mine. And if I . . .

BR JASPER. Lord Boreal, I'm confused. There are, to my certain knowledge, only two alethiometers in the whole of the Church's empire. There's the one in my hand, and there's Lyra Belacqua's.

LORD BOREAL. This is it. It's hers!

PRESIDENT. How did it get to you?

LORD BOREAL. The boy had it. He and Lyra are travelling together. They're inseparable.

Agitated discussion breaks out.

PRESIDENT. Silence!

There's quiet, and all eyes are now on the PRESIDENT, *who is thoughtful.*

It's very troubling that the boy and the girl have met. One feels a pattern behind it . . . an intelligence, almost. And it brings me directly to the reason why I've summoned this Council. Brother Jasper, tell our friends in holiness what you have just discovered.

BROTHER JASPER *rises.*

BR JASPER. Ever since Lyra Belacqua was born, it has been known that she's the child in the witches' prophecy, the child who will either redeem the Church or bring about the triumph of Dust, one or the other. The answer to this riddle could be found only in a secret name, a name which has eluded the Church for a full twelve years . . . and which the alethiometer has now revealed.

All listen in great suspense.

That name is Eve, the mother of us all, the fount of original sin, and the cause of Dust's invasion of the world. The Triumph of Dust.

As this news is heard, the NUNS *and* CLERICS *fall to their knees, pray and wail in terrible distress.*

PRESIDENT. Lord Boreal, Fate has delivered this child into your hands. When you see her tonight, you will eliminate her.

LORD BOREAL. I shall.

PRESIDENT. The Church will provide you with absolution in advance for the taking of two human lives.

LORD BOREAL. *Two*?

PRESIDENT. Yes, two! We can't let the boy survive.

LORD BOREAL. Of course not, no, I'm sorry.

PRESIDENT. You must not fail. If they escape you alive, they'll flee to Cittàgazze, where no adult can pursue them. And we sadly can't wipe out our enemies at a distance.

BROTHER JASPER *speaks quietly in the* PRESIDENT'*s ear.*

Send him in.

BROTHER JASPER *goes out.*

One last point. Mrs Coulter doesn't know that you've found her daughter, does she?

LORD BOREAL. She does. I've told her. In fact she's going back to Oxford with me tonight, in order to take Lyra into her care. I thought you'd promised her that she could. I hope I've not done wrong.

Everyone looks at him in the interesting expectation of his being sentenced to death.

PRESIDENT. I think, on balance, that this could be an interesting test of Mrs Coulter's loyalty. Stick to the plan, and if her maternal feelings start getting the better of her, you'll just have to kill her as well.

LORD BOREAL. Of course.

PRESIDENT. You may go.

LORD BOREAL *goes, as* BROTHER JASPER *shows in* DR SARGENT. *He's pale and trembling, and his clothes are creased and torn.*

Brother Jasper tells me that your field of expertise could be of use to us.

DR SARGENT. So I hope . . . my name is Sargent, Dr
Sargent? I'm currently under interrogation as part of the
war-effort . . . but I was, in happier times, the leader of Mrs
Coulter's scientific team at Bolvangar . . .

Some sceptical titters and sneers.

. . . an unfortunate project, I admit. But what we learned
there . . .

PRESIDENT. Get to the point.

DR SARGENT. You wish to eliminate an enemy in a different
world, is that correct? I know how it could be done. Of
course I'd need a fully-equipped laboratory . . .

PRESIDENT. You shall have one. We shall omit nothing that
might help us in our struggle against Dust. If that means
destroying the Holy Church itself, so let it be. But better a
world with neither Church nor Dust than a world unworthy
of its divine Creator. Go in peace.

The air over Cittàgazze. The WITCHES *are flying.*

SERAFINA. Fly on, sisters!

PIPISTRELLE. I've seen no sign of the child.

WITCHES. Nor me! Nor me!

SERAFINA. But she's here in Cittàgazze. That we know.
Jopari told us. Fly on!

WITCHES. Fly on! Fly on!

WILL*'s Oxford. Night.* WILL *and* LYRA *at the iron gate to*
LORD BOREAL*'s house. It's locked shut.* LYRA *rattles the
gate.*

LYRA. What do you think?

WILL. Let's try.

*He uses the knife to cut through the gate, and they go
through.*

There's the house. Hang on.

LYRA. Is your hand still hurting?

WILL. Yes, and it's bleeding like anything. Do up the bandage, will you?

She starts doing so.

LYRA. I did this.

WILL. Yeah, well shut up about it.

LYRA. I did. You'd never have fought that man if I hadn't pushed you into it. 'Cause I wanted the alethiometer back, and I shouldn't've done. I'm meant to be helping you find your dad.

WILL. Well you forgot for a minute. Let's get on with what we're doing.

LYRA. We don't have to. We could knock on Lord Boreal's door and give him the knife.

WILL. Then he'll have *both* our things. Look, it's all decided. We'll keep the knife, and we'll burgle his house and take the alethiometer.

LYRA. How?

WILL. You stay here. Then I'll cut a window from this world into Cittàgazze, and I'll walk to where I think his study is, cut into it and grab the alethiometer, then I'll jump back into Cittàgazze-world, run back here, you come through, and I'll close up the window. Got it?

LYRA. You're gonna cut into another world, walk along a bit and cut back into this one?

WILL. Yeah.

LYRA. While I stay here?

WILL. That's it. Don't bother me now. If I think about anything else, the knife's gonna break, remember? Take this.

He gives LYRA *the green leather writing-case.*

And Pan, you better get out of sight.

PANTALAIMON. I was expecting that.

WILL cuts a window.

WILL. I won't be a minute.

He goes through. LYRA hears something, then hides as LORD BOREAL and MRS COULTER appear. LORD BOREAL is carrying the alethiometer.

LYRA. Will!

She goes through the window after him. LORD BOREAL and MRS COULTER approach the house.

MRS COULTER. So this is your secret world? It's charming.

LORD BOREAL. I hardly believe its charm is what made you insist that I brought you here.

MRS COULTER. Of course it isn't. I want my daughter. I won't be sharing a room with her, I hope?

LORD BOREAL. No, certainly not. I asked my manservant to make up the guest-room for you.

MRS COULTER. The guest-room? Well, we mustn't upset him. I must remember to rumple the sheets in the morning. You really are the most delightfully old-fashioned host.

They go into the house. We see WILL, about to cut a window. LYRA appears behind him.

LYRA. Will!

WILL. What are you doing? I told you to stay out there.

LYRA. He's back, and he's brought my mum! If she finds me, I'm done for!

WILL. Ssh!

He cuts a window, and finds himself looking down through the ceiling into LORD BOREAL's living-room.

LYRA. Why are we in the ceiling?

WILL. I've cut into it too high up. The ground level must be different or something.

LORD BOREAL *is heard outside.*

LORD BOREAL. One moment.

WILL. Ssh!

LORD BOREAL *comes in.* WILL *and* LYRA *watch as he puts down the alethiometer-box, quickly opens a drawer, takes out a revolver, checks it and puts it back.*

LYRA. Look at that!

MRS COULTER *comes in with* THE GOLDEN MONKEY.

MRS COULTER. Now you are quite certain that Lyra's coming?

LORD BOREAL. Without a doubt. She wants her pretty piece of clockwork.

She opens the box and looks at it.

MRS COULTER. You won't *really* give it back to her, will you?

LORD BOREAL. Oh no. Although I'm sure she'll scream and shout and cause an appalling scene.

MRS COULTER. She'll learn to behave once I've got her under lock and key, I can assure you of that.

She hands it back to him.

LYRA. Bloody old cow.

MRS COULTER. You're perspiring, Charles.

LORD BOREAL. It's often a little warmer in this world than one is dressed for. May I offer you a glass of sherry?

MRS COULTER. I'll have one if you do.

He goes to pour drinks.

How did you find her?

LORD BOREAL. Lyra? She arrived with the boy.

MRS COULTER. And where did *he* spring from?

LORD BOREAL. I found him in town, in the cuttings library. We were both looking up the identical file, and it occurred to me in a flash that he could get me the knife.

MRS COULTER. Why?

LORD BOREAL. Because, being a child, he won't be devoured by the Spectres. And he's a murderer.

MRS COULTER. A *murderer*?

LORD BOREAL. My dear, he's twelve years old, and he's already killed a highly-trained secret service operative. Oh yes, a very bad hat. On drugs, I imagine . . . single mother living on state handouts . . .

WILL. Bastard!

MRS COULTER. Well, that's typical of Lyra. Even at Jordan, she used to find her playmates in the gutter. We had one of her friends at Bolvangar, a beastly little kitchen-boy, called Roddy or Rudy . . .

They drink.

LYRA. I'll kill her!

WILL. Calm down! I want you to go back into Oxford, come round the outside of the house and chuck a couple of stones at the window, so they go running outside, all right? I'll grab the alethiometer and run.

LYRA. Yeah, all right. I'm still gonna kill her.

She goes. In the living-room, the MONKEY *is looking inquiringly at the drawer with the revolver inside.*

MRS COULTER. But she's my daughter, Charles. I'll guard and protect her till I die. I want you to know that particularly.

LORD BOREAL. Why me?

MRS COULTER. Because you're keeping something back, I know you are. What's in that drawer?

He glances back at the drawer.

LORD BOREAL. What drawer?

MRS COULTER. The one you keep looking at.

LORD BOREAL. I don't!

MRS COULTER. You do. Besides, your story doesn't make
    sense. Why were you and the boy looking up the identical
    file in the same cuttings library? What's the link?

    WILL *listens intently.*

LORD BOREAL. His father.

MRS COULTER. Well?

LORD BOREAL. Twelve years ago, John Parry, soldier and
    Arctic explorer, discovered a window between the worlds
    and walked through it into Cittàgazze. My friends in the
    secret services have been trying to find that window for
    years. It has profound intelligence implications . . .

MRS COULTER. The *link!* The *link!*

LORD BOREAL. I'm coming to that. Parry is still alive, in
    hiding, under a different name . . . the name that was given
    him by the Northern tribesmen when he . . .

    A handful of stones clatters against a glass window.

MRS COULTER. It's them, it must be!

    LORD BOREAL *takes the revolver out of the drawer.*

    Charles! What are you doing?

    He runs out. WILL *prepares to climb down into the room.*
    MRS COULTER *runs out after* LORD BOREAL *and they
    struggle. A shot is fired into the air.* THE GOLDEN
    MONKEY *trips* LORD BOREAL *up and he falls, winded.*
    LYRA *can be seen, waiting by the gate for* WILL.

    Lyra! Lyra! Look out my darling!

    WILL *appears in the knife-cut window, carrying the
    alethiometer.*

WILL. Over here!

    He slashes at the MONKEY*'s face, pulls* LYRA *through
    and closes the window.* LORD BOREAL *struggles to his*

feet with the gun in his hand, and stares at the place where
the window disappeared.

LORD BOREAL. It works!

MRS COULTER. It certainly does. And what was the gun for,
Charles?

LORD BOREAL. For the boy, of course. I have my orders.

MRS COULTER. Then you'd better go after him.

LORD BOREAL. What, follow him into Cittàgazze? I can't go
there. The Spectres would suck the soul clean out of my
body . . .

MRS COULTER. What if you had no soul? You've little
enough. I'm joking, Charles . . . but now that I think of it . . .
if the Spectres are after Dust . . . which it seems they are,
since they've no interest in children . . . . then there might
be a way of giving them what they want without being
killed oneself. We'll go in the morning.

LORD BOREAL. We?

MRS COULTER. Yes, we. Do you think I could bear to search
for my daughter quite this far, and then see only a glimpse
of her? We'll wake up early, and we'll find that window by
the bus shelter. Then we'll explore.

Cittàgazze. WILL *lies collapsed on the ground, exhausted and*
in pain. LYRA *is with him.*

WILL. He was talking about my dad. He said he found a
window. Just like me. And he's *alive.*

LYRA. Ssh . . . Let's talk in the morning. We'll go to the place
we met. I'll cook an omelette . . .

WILL *is asleep.*

He's asleep.

PANTALAIMON. Why do you think his father's so important?

LYRA. Dunno.

PANTALAIMON. Where d'you think he is?

LYRA. I don't know!

PANTALAIMON. You could ask the alethiometer.

LYRA. Oh Pan, you heard what he said in Oxford. I can't go snooping on him.

PANTALAIMON. That makes a change. It used to be you who was always snooping, and me who tried to stop you.

LYRA. I know . . . but I think I'm changing. If we hadn't gone snooping in the Retiring Room, do you think any of this would have happened?

PANTALAIMON. Not in *this* world. But there could be another world where your father drank the poison . . .

LYRA. . . . yeah . . . or where the gyptians never found me . . .

PANTALAIMON. . . . or the Gobblers cut us.

LYRA. . . . or where Roger's alive.

SERAFINA *appears*.

SERAFINA. Lyra!

LYRA. Serafina Pekkala! What are you doing here?

SERAFINA. We've been searching for you throughout this world. Who is this boy?

LYRA. It's Will. He's sick. He had two of his fingers cut off with a knife.

SERAFINA. I saw it. It's the reason that I could come to land. There are Spectres spread in a circle all around us, but they'll come no nearer. They fear that knife.

She walks round WILL, *looking at him*.

He's a good-looking fellow, don't you think?

LYRA. Is he?

SERAFINA. There's some would think so. My sisters will be here in a trice, so tell me quickly. What is he like?

LYRA. He's brave. He's good.

SERAFINA. Do you trust him?

LYRA. Yeah, I do . . . but why're you asking me all these
  questions?

SERAFINA. It's hard for a witch to know what a short-lived
  girl like you might feel for a boy. We live so long, you see,
  for hundreds of years, never aging, never changing . . . and
  men are quite the opposite. They're like butterflies, dead by
  nightfall. We no sooner fall in love with them, than they're
  gone. We bear their children, who are witches if they are
  girls . . . but mortals like their fathers if they are boys . . .
  and then we watch our sons growing strong and golden and
  handsome, knowing all the time that they'll die of old age,
  or on the battlefield, while we're still young, while we're
  still bearing son after son, each one of them just as doomed
  as the ones before. And finally our hearts are broken.

LYRA. Was Farder Coram in love with you?

SERAFINA. He was, and I loved him. I'd fallen to earth in the
  Fenland marshes, where Coram was fishing, and he hauled
  me into his boat, or I'd have drowned. He was twenty and
  I was pushing two hundred . . . Well, I lay a week in his
  cabin, with the light blocked out, while I was mending from
  my fall. But it was summer outside, and the light was
  calling. One afternoon we strolled across the fields. We
  picked fruits from the hedgerows . . . we sat, we talked, we
  watched the river . . . and I lifted a blackberry and pressed
  it against his lips. It was only then that I knew I loved him.
  Nine months later, I bore his child . . .

LYRA. Was it a girl, a witch?

SERAFINA. He was a boy, and he died very young, in the
  great fever. It tore a piece out of my heart, and Coram was
  broken by it. I would have stayed and cared for him, but
  I had to fly back to the North to be Queen of my clan.
  I hoped that he would forget me, and find a human wife.

LYRA. He never did.

SERAFINA. I know that now. It seems that our destinies were
  bound together after all, like yours and this boy's may be.

WITCHES *appear.*

WITCHES. Serafina Pekkala! / We're here! / Have you found the child?

SERAFINA. Not so loud. There's a young man sleeping.

The WITCHES *look at* WILL *with great interest.*

We'll guard and guide these children wherever they wish to go. So tell us, Lyra, where are you heading for?

LYRA. We're looking for Will's dad. But we don't even know where to start.

SERAFINA. Can your alethiometer not help you?

LYRA. He told me not to ask it.

PANTALAIMON. But us and him are together, aren't we? Ask it where *we* oughta go. Then it won't be snooping.

LYRA. Well . . . just this once.

She consults the alethiometer.

We've got to travel to those blue mountains across the bay . . . and we gotta go fast. My mum's coming after me.

LORD ASRIEL*'s fortress. On the battlefield. Military preparations are in progress.* LORD ASRIEL *addresses his troops.*

LORD ASRIEL. I stepped through the Aurora. I travelled through world after world, each one of them stranger and less familiar than the one before, until I'd found the limit that man can reach, a world beyond which lies only the spirit-domain of the Authority. And it's into this world, this final outpost of reality, that we shall tempt him. My fortress tempts him, poised on a spike of rock, visible for a hundred miles around, like a naked challenge. You tempt him, men, spirits, angels, streaming towards the battlefield, piercing the barriers that kept us in ignorance of each other. But what tempts him most of all is what has brought us together. Our refusal to submit. Our resistance. Our will to be free.

He cannot allow that. He has to attack it. His pride will
accept no less. He will invade this world, and then we can
fight him, just as the brightest and most beloved of all the
angels fought him at the dawn of time. But there's a
difference now. There is a knife, 'Æsahættr', celebrated in
the Norsk legends, seen by Gilgamesh in a dream, foretold
by the Delphic oracle to Alexander the Great. A knife so
sharp, so keenly-edged that it can pierce his heart as though
it were human flesh. We shall have that knife. We will
defeat the Authority. We shall topple him from his throne.
We shall destroy him.

Applause. LORD ASRIEL *and* STELMARIA *are left alone.*

STELMARIA. Fine words.

LORD ASRIEL. Be quiet.

STELMARIA. Why did you boast about the knife? You
haven't got it.

LORD ASRIEL. Jopari will send it. He's a man of honour.

STELMARIA. And what about Lyra?

LORD ASRIEL. Lyra? She's got nothing to do with this.

STELMARIA. Then why is she in danger from the Church?

LORD ASRIEL. I don't believe she is. That was just her
mother's excuse for abandoning me.

STELMARIA. What about the zeppelin they sent after her?

LORD ASRIEL *registers this. An* OFFICER *appears.*

OFFICER. My lord, the chief of the Gallivespians has arrived.

LORD ROKE, *a Gallivespian, appears flying on a dragon-
fly.*

LORD ROKE. Good day, your lordship.

LORD ASRIEL. Lord Roke, what excellent timing.

LORE ROKE *dismounts.*

LORD ROKE. A stirring speech, your lordship. We
Gallivespians are right behind you. How can I help?

LORD ASRIEL. Since time immemorial, Lord Roke, brave
Gallivespians like yourself have crept through keyholes,
hidden in cupboards, lurked in the pockets of coats to discover the secrets which we blundering humans can't find out.

LORD ROKE. Are these kind remarks the prelude to some
risky assignment?

LORD ASRIEL. They may be. Won't you perch on my hand?

LORD ROKE. A singular honour.

He sits on LORD ASRIEL's *hand.*

LORD ASRIEL. What have you heard about the Church's
policy towards my daughter?

LORD ROKE. They believe her to be a serious menace. But
I don't know why.

LORD ASRIEL. Then we'd better find out. I want you to send
your two most trusted spies to the Consistorial Court of
Discipline in Geneva. They will report to me daily by
lodestone resonator. I want every detail, every hint of
information they can provide about the Church's attempts to
find her, and their reason for doing so.

LORD ROKE. May I suggest the Chevalier Tialys and his
spouse, the Lady Salmakia? They work very well as a team.

LORD ASRIEL. Whoever you wish.

LORD ROKE. I can't help feeling that the god-destroying
knife will feature high on the Church's scale of interest. Do
you wish to be kept informed?

LORD ASRIEL. The knife's been taken care of.

STELMARIA. But be sure that your spies include it in their
reports.

Cittàgazze. The Torre degli Angeli. MRS COULTER *and*
LORD BOREAL *are dragging* GIACOMO PARADISI *out of
the door. He's moaning and whimpering with terror.* BOREAL
is also terrified.

MRS COULTER. Spectres! I've brought you a gift! Isn't that what you want? Aren't you hungry?

PARADISI *looks in horror as the* SPECTRES *approach him.* CHILDREN, *including* PAOLO *and* ANGELICA, *appear and watch with unhealthy interest.*

Charles! Watch!

PARADISI *flails his hands in the air, then turns to the tower and obsessively examines the stonework. His movements slow down, then stop. He stands, lifeless and frozen.* MRS COULTER *inspects him.*

Total removal of the soul . . . just like Bolvangar. Stop whimpering, Charles! They've gone.

LORD BOREAL. Marisa . . . never, ever, put me through anything like this again.

MRS COULTER. We're in no danger! The Spectres and I have reached an understanding. I find them souls, and in return they'll leave us alone. As soon as you described them to me, I knew that I could dominate them, and so it turned out. Children, stay. This gentleman has a question for you.

To LORD BOREAL:

Go on!

LORD BOREAL. My dears, we're looking for a boy and a girl of about your age. Have you seen them?

PAOLO. Yeah.

ANGELICA. They're vile.

PAOLO. They're evil.

LORD BOREAL. Did the boy have a knife, when you saw him last?

ANGELICA. Yeah, he stole it from our brother Tullio.

PAOLO. Then Tullio got eaten by the Spectres, just like this old geezer.

ANGELICA. Except we wasn't laughing that time.

MRS COULTER. No, I'm sure you weren't. Where did they
   go, this boy and girl?

PAOLO. Up to the mountains, there, with lots of flying ladies.

ANGELICA. When you find the kids, will you kill 'em for us?

PAOLO. *Please!*

MRS COULTER. Carry our bags until we're out of the city,
   and we might consider it. And if you're really good, I'll
   give you a present. Do you like chocolatl?

Cittàgazze. In the mountains. Evening. The WITCHES, LYRA,
WILL *and* PANTALAIMON *are on trek.* WILL *is nursing his
hand. It's cold and they're all wrapped up.* SERAFINA *gives
out orders.*

SERAFINA. Stop! This is where we'll rest for the night. Four
   of you stay in the air to keep a lookout.

GRIMHILD. What for?

CAITLIN. The Spectres won't come near us, not while the
   knife's about.

SERAFINA. There may be other dangers. You there, make a
   fire. You and you, get busy skinning our supper.

   The WITCHES *get busy. Thunder.* SERAFINA *looks up at
   the sky.*

   It's going to rain.

LYRA. Come on, Will. We'll all snuggle up together.

   He sits with her.

   Put my blanket around you.

   They wrap up together.

   Here, Pan! You're getting left out.

   WILL *lifts a corner of blanket next to him for*
   PANTALAIMON, *who pointedly goes the long way round
   to* LYRA's *side and gets in with her.*

He's never gonna touch you, Will. That's one of the rules.

WILL. I wish I had a daemon.

PANTALAIMON. You *have*.

LYRA. He's right. We're both human, aren't we? It wouldn't make sense if you didn't have one.

WILL. Then why can't I see it?

LYRA. 'Cause it's inside you.

WILL. So there's daemons in my world?

LYRA. Yup.

WILL. It could be true. 'Cause I think there's Spectres there as well.

LYRA. What makes you think that?

WILL. Well . . . you remember what Tullio did, when the Spectres got him?

LYRA. Yeah, he got sorta interested in little tiny things, like the stones in the wall. What about it?

WILL. My mum does that. I haven't told you much about her. I've not told anyone, really. She gets ill, like ill in her head, with worry and fear. She'll count the railings in the park, or the leaves on a bush or the tins in a supermarket. As though she's turning away from something that frightens her. There's plenty of real things for her to be frightened of. My dad never coming back, or the men who were after his letters. But it's more than that. It's things that nobody else can see. Maybe they're the same as Spectres, only in my world we call them something else. Like mad, or looney.

LYRA. Did you always want to find your dad?

WILL. Yeah, always. I used to pretend he was a prisoner in a dungeon, and I'd help him escape. Or a castaway on a desert island, and I'd be the captain of the boat that rescued him. I imagined him saying, 'Well done, my son. No-one on earth could have done better. I'm proud of you.' My mother used to say I was gonna wear his mantle.

LYRA. What's a mantle?

WILL. It's a task, a purpose. But I could never wear my dad's in a million years. He was a soldier, a fighter.

LYRA. You fought Tullio.

WILL. I had to, didn't I? Don't think I liked it.

LYRA. When I was at Jordan, I used to fight all the time, and I never been so happy in all my life. Did you not fight ever?

WILL. Just once. It was one of my mum's bad times. She went out of the house not properly dressed. Well, hardly dressed. There were some boys from school got hold of her, and they tormented her. Tortured her mentally. I got her home and I got so angry with her. She said, 'Will, what are you doing?'

LYRA. What did she mean?

WILL. 'Will, what're you doing? What're you doing?' It's obvious. I was shouting at her, and she didn't understand a single thing that was happening. Well, the next day at school, I found the boy who'd started it all. I broke his arm and I knocked out some of his teeth. Then afterwards I had to pretend I was sorry. The other kids all shut up about it. They knew that I'd kill them if they said anything that meant I got put into care, or my mum got taken away. After that, I lived a normal life. Had a couple of friends, even. But I never trusted kids again. They're just as keen as grown-ups to do bad things.

RUTA SKADI *appears.*

RUTA SKADI. Sisters! Take cover! There's a storm approaching!

WITCHES. Ruta Skadi! Welcome! Where have you been?

They welcome her to ground noisily.

RUTA SKADI. Bring me food.

A WITCH goes to get food.

I flew with the angels! Great beings of light, all shining, older than time. They talked to me, but I was too young to understand them. Give me that.

She grabs food and eats ravenously, standing up.

I saw Lord Asriel! He asked us to join him! To fight on his side! Wouldn't you rather *that*, sisters, than sit on your arses skinning rabbits? Come with me! Fly to the battlefield!

There's a chorus of agreement from the WITCHES*:*

GRENDELLA. I will!

CAITLIN. I'll come too!

GRIMHILD. Can't we go there, Serafina Pekkala?

SERAFINA. No we can't, and you all know why! Let me talk to our sister.

The WITCHES *disperse.* SERAFINA *and* RUTA SKADI *talk where they can't be overheard.*

The prophecy's coming true. We've found the girl, and she's travelling with a boy. Lyra, come here.

LYRA *approaches.*

LYRA. Did you really meet my father?

RUTA SKADI. If you could see him . . . ! He's built a fortress, Lyra, with turrets rearing up to the skies, and roads across the plains bringing him gunpowder, cannons, armour-plate. There's fighters joining him . . . humans, lizards and apes, huge birds with poisonous spurs . . . and witches from all the worlds! *Men*-witches too!

SERAFINA. You're making it up!

RUTA SKADI *sees* WILL.

RUTA SKADI. Who's that?

LYRA. It's Will.

RUTA SKADI *recognises the name.*

RUTA SKADI. Come into the light.

WILL *comes nearer. He looks weaker and very ill. To* SERAFINA*:*

What's wrong with his hand?

SERAFINA. It's a spirit-wound. Our spells can't heal it. The plants and herbs are all quite different in this world.

To LYRA *and* WILL:

Go back to sleep.

They do.

RUTA SKADI. I've seen those eyes before.

PIPISTRELLE *calls over, pointing upwards.*

PIPISTRELLE. Serafina Pekkala! There's a balloon being blown like a sea-bird through the skies!

WITCHES *look up and clamour.* RUTA SKADI *looks up with growing emotion.*

WITCHES. Who's inside it? / Is it him?

GRIMHILD. It's Jopari! It's Jopari with the Texan.

GRENDELLA. Look! Look! There's two Church zeppelins on his tail!

There's a flash and a huge crash of thunder.

CAITLIN. They're caught in the storm . . .

PIPISTRELLE. . . . the lightning flashes . . .

GRIMHILD. . . . and the thunder rolls . . .

PIPISTRELLE. . . . and there's one of them struck!

Cheers. Flames are seen in the sky.

GRIMHILD. It's burning! It's burning!

CAITLIN. It's down in flames, and there's just one zeppelin left to do the Church's dirty work!

GRENDELLA. Where's Jopari?

PIPISTRELLE. He's flying high!

WITCHES. He's flying! He's flying! / Jopari is safe!

The WITCHES *cheer and sing a chant of triumph.* RUTA SKADI *turns furiously to* SERAFINA.

RUTA SKADI. Why is Jopari in this world?

SERAFINA. I don't know! He was meant to have gone back home.

RUTA SKADI. But why did you bring him here at all? I have to kill him now. You know I must kill him. Why didn't you join the war? Or stay in the Arctic, where you could do no harm?

SERAFINA. Don't make me angry, Ruta Skadi. You know very well, that all I have cared about, since that child came into our lives, is that the prophecy comes true.

RUTA SKADI. Then *let* it. Let it come true, or let it fail, if that's what destiny chooses. We're destiny's children, we're not its nursemaids. Lyra must do what she does of her own free will. Leave her alone!

Cittàgazze. MRS COULTER*'s camp.* MRS COULTER *and* LORD BOREAL. *He still has his gun. She's at ease, writing a letter. He's edgy. She looks up and listens.*

MRS COULTER. When the thunder stops, I can hear the singing of the witches. Aren't you excited?

LORD BOREAL. I must confess, Marisa, that what's mostly absorbing my attention is the sight of those Spectres hovering in that copse of trees.

MRS COULTER. Yes, I'll have to find someone to give them soon. It's just a shame those ghastly children weren't a little bit older. I've been thinking, Charles, what a very good team we are. I needed you to guide me here. You needed me to survive.

LORD BOREAL. Quite true.

MRS COULTER. What will you do, when we find the witches?

LORD BOREAL. I'll get the knife, and hurry back to Geneva as fast as my legs will take me. What about you?

MRS COULTER. I'll keep my daughter . . . quiet and safe. That's all I want. When she lived with me in London, I used to sit at the end of her bed and watch her, and my heart would burst with love. Then she'd wake up and . . . oh . . . the racketing round and the noise and nuisance. I'd have to remind myself of what she was like before, and then I'd love her again. What's odd is that I still don't know the most important thing about her.

LORD BOREAL. What might that be?

MRS COULTER. Oh, Charles. We've grown so close in the last few days. You can't imagine that I've not suspected.

LORD BOREAL. Suspected what?

MRS COULTER. That you know her secret name.

LORD BOREAL. What name?

MRS COULTER. Stop treating me like a fool. It's something bad, it's a name that they won't allow. That's why you were going to kill her. Isn't that true?

LORD BOREAL. Really, my dear . . .

MRS COULTER. I'm serious, Charles. I tortured a witch to get that name. They'd tied her up in a chair. I broke her fingers, one by one . . . and I'll do worse to you! I insist you tell me! What is that name?

LORD BOREAL. Marisa, my dear, believe me . . .

MRS COULTER. Spectres! Take him!

The SPECTRES *advance.*

LORD BOREAL. Don't! I beg you! Send them away!

MRS COULTER (*to the* SPECTRES). Stop! (*To* LORD BOREAL.) Well?

LORD BOREAL. The name is Eve. The Lady Eve. The wife of Adam, and the cause of the first great Fall.

MRS COULTER. You lied to me! You spy! You double-dealer!

She snaps her fingers. The SPECTRES *advance and devour* LORD BOREAL, *as he cries out.*

LORD BOREAL. No! Keep away! Marisa, help me! Help me!

He falls silent and lifeless. She takes the gun from his hand.

MRS COULTER. Eve. Why didn't I guess? It was too big for me to see. And there's a boy. An Adam. As before, so now again. But this time, Eve will die. Unless I save her.

The WITCHES' *camp. Moonlight. The* WITCHES *are sleeping.* LYRA *and* WILL *are lying on the ground.* SERAFINA *approaches.*

SERAFINA. Lyra.

PANTALAIMON. She's asleep.

SERAFINA. I must go. Ruta Skadi has left in a rage, and I'm terrified of what she might do. Tell Will to get some sleep. I know it's difficult for him.

She goes.

WILL. Pan. Look at my hand.

He shows his hand, which is bleeding, septic and gangrenous.

It's worse than ever. I never knew anything could hurt so much. The blood's gushing out of it, and it's bad, it's smelling. Am I going to die? I'm so frightened.

PANTALAIMON *licks his hand.*

What are you doing?

PANTALAIMON. Lyra doesn't think you're frightened. She thinks you're the bravest fighter she's ever seen. She thinks you're as brave as Iorek Byrnison.

LYRA *opens her eyes and listens.*

WILL. She's braver than me. She's the best friend I ever had.

PANTALAIMON. She thinks that about you as well.

WILL. What would she think of me if I died like this? In the middle of nowhere . . . on a stupid search for a dad who went through a window and vanished . . .

PANTALAIMON. He's still alive.

WILL. He didn't bother to come home, though, did he? I've been lying here trying to think what to do. But the pain's so bad, and I get so muddled.

He stands.

I'm going for a walk.

He goes. LYRA *sits up.*

LYRA. You licked his hand.

PANTALAIMON. I felt sorry for him.

LYRA. Shall I go after him?

PANTALAIMON. No, don't. He wants to be on his own.

LYRA. He said I was the best friend he ever had. What if that's the last thing I ever hear him say?

PANTALAIMON. It'll be the last thing and the best.

LYRA. Yeah.

THE GOLDEN MONKEY *appears and creeps towards her.* MRS COULTER *appears.* LYRA *sees it and springs up.*

MRS COULTER. Lyra, it's me.

LYRA. Go away!

MRS COULTER. Don't be afraid. I'm taking you back to our own world, darling, to our beautiful world of daemons. Come to your mother.

LYRA. Will! Will!

The WITCHES *awake in a great commotion.*

WITCHES. It's her! / The torturing-woman! / Wake up! / Seize her! / Kill her!

They draw their bows and arrows. MRS COULTER *turns away, hands upraised.*

MRS COULTER. Spectres! Now for the feast!

SPECTRES *appear out of the darkness and attack the* WITCHES. *They shudder and struggle as their souls are devoured.* LYRA *screams to* WILL *for help.* MRS COULTER *and* THE GOLDEN MONKEY *carry her away.*

Cittàgazze. On the mountain. There's a rock in the shape of a standing bear. WILL *appears, in great pain.* JOPARI *appears out of the darkness.*

JOPARI. Give me your hand.

    WILL *stares at him.*

WILL. Who are you?

JOPARI. Give it to me.

    Cautiously, WILL *holds out his hand.* JOPARI *takes out a little flask and puts ointment on it.*

    I came to this world to look for an old, old man. And he sent me to you . . . and I discover you're just a child. Well, so it must be. Don't move.

    He takes WILL*'s bandage and throws it away.*

    There.

WILL. It's stopped hurting. Even the bleeding's stopped.

JOPARI. Have you got the knife?

WILL. Who are you?

JOPARI. It doesn't matter. Are you carrying it with you now?

WILL. Yes.

JOPARI. Show it to me.

    WILL *does.* JOPARI *examines it and gives it back to* WILL.

    You think you chose this knife. Or that you stumbled across it. Wrong. It chose you. If you don't use it now to fight the forces of evil, it will be torn from you and used against the rest of the human race, for all eternity.

WILL. Forget it, will you? I'm not gonna fight. I hate fighting.

JOPARI. Did you fight to get it?

WILL. Yes.

JOPARI. And did you win it in single combat?

WILL. Yes.

JOPARI. Then you're a fighter. You're a warrior. Argue with
me if you like, but don't argue against your own nature.
Now listen. There are two great powers, and they've been
enemies ever since time began. There's the power that wants
us to obey and be humble and submit, and the power that
wants us to know more, and be wiser and stronger. Every
advance in human life, every scrap of knowledge and
wisdom and decency has been torn by one side from the
teeth of the other. Now those two powers are lining up in
battle. Each of them needs that knife. You have to choose.
We've both been guided to this place, this night, this
moment . . . you with the knife, and me to tell you what you
must do with it.

WILL. You're wrong! I know what I'm doing. I'm searching,
right? And it's not for the knife. It's . . .

JOPARI. Your search is over. You found what you were *meant*
to find. Now you must take it to Lord Asriel . . .

WILL. I thought he was evil.

JOPARI. Don't talk about things you know nothing about. Tell
him that this is the weapon he needs above all others,
'Æsahættr'. Set off at once. Ignore everything else, no
matter how important it may seem. Guides will show you
the way. The night is full of angels. Wait. I'll never meet
you again. I'm dying. Let me see what you look like.

He strikes a match. They stare at each other.

You're my son. You're Will.

WILL. Dad?

An arrow strikes JOPARI *and he falls dead.* RUTA SKADI
is there, bow in hand.

What have you done? I looked for him all my life, and now you've killed him.

RUTA SKADI. I loved him. And he rejected me, for the sake of your mother and you! I am a witch! I don't forgive! I can't forgive!

She stabs herself and dies. WILL *goes to his* FATHER.

WILL. Dad. Dad, you loved us. I'm sorry I doubted you. I'll do what you want, I swear it. I'll be the man that you want me to be. I'll fight. I'll be a warrior. I'll take this knife to Lord Asriel, wherever he is. You can rest now. You can sleep.

He stands. Very faintly, in the far distance, LYRA *can be heard screaming.*

Lyra?

He walks, then runs back to the WITCHES' *encampment. He passes* WITCHES, *dead and frozen. He runs faster.*

Lyra! Lyra!

He finds the place where he and LYRA *were sleeping. She has gone.*

Oh God. Oh God. She's gone.

He finds SERAFINA, *convulsed with despair.* KAISA *is also there.*

SERAFINA. It was the woman with the monkey-daemon. She killed my witches.

KAISA. All of them, all of them.

WILL. Where's Lyra?

SERAFINA. Her mother has taken her, Will. I arrived too late. Where were you?

WILL. I found my dad. And now he's dead. But he gave me a task. I've got to take this knife to Lord Asriel.

SERAFINA. So the choice is yours. Either save the world, or
save your friend. I know which I would do. But I can't help
you to decide. Ruta Skadi was right. I meddled in human
lives, and brought destruction on my sisters. If all goes well
for you and Lyra, we'll meet on the battlefield. Farewell.

She embraces him and goes. WILL *picks up* LYRA's *ruck-
sack. Feels the presence of the alethiometer and takes it out.
Looks at it.*

WILL. Which should I choose?

Two angels – BALTHAMOS *and* BARUCH *– appear.*

Who are you?

BALTHAMOS. We are angels. We have been following your
father. We hoped he would lead us to you . . .

BARUCH. . . . and he did.

WILL. Why didn't you save him?

BARUCH. We protected him all the time until he found you.

BALTHAMOS. Then his task was over. Now we must lead you
to Lord Asriel.

WILL *hesitates.*

What are you waiting for?

WILL. I'll do that later.

He holds out the alethiometer.

I want you to help me to find the girl that this belongs to.

BARUCH. Have you forgotten your father's orders?

BALTHAMOS. You must ignore everything else, never mind
how important it might seem.

WILL. Are you stronger than me, or weaker?

BALTHAMOS. Weaker. You've got flesh. We're only made of
spirit.

WILL. Right, then I'm telling you. Help me to find her.

BALTHAMOS. Ask us politely and we may.

WILL. Do you know where her mother's taken her?

BARUCH. We know where she came from.

BALTHAMOS. From a tent nearby with a dead man eaten by Spectres.

WILL. What does he look like?

BARUCH. Pasty. Silvery hair. Sixty.

WILL. She's killed Lord Boreal. That's something good. One of you follow her, fast as you can. Come back and tell me where they've gone. The other one stay.

BARUCH. You are making a great mistake . . .

BALTHAMOS. . . . but we have no choice.

A cave. Red silk prayer-scarves, a waterfall, a rainbow. LYRA *is asleep.* ROGER'S GHOST *appears.*

ROGER. Lyra? Can you hear me?

LYRA *stirs in her sleep, then half-wakes up.*

LYRA. Roger, where are you? Roger!

MRS COULTER *comes in, carrying a bowl containing a sleeping-draught. She hurries to* LYRA *and feeds her with a spoon.*

MRS COULTER. Don't be upset, my darling, it's only a dream. I've brought your medicine. It will keep you calm, it'll keep you sleeping.

LYRA *goes back to sleep.*

How lovely you look. Are you happy like this? I am.

Cittàgazze. MRS COULTER's *camp.* WILL *is putting things in a bag.* LORD BOREAL *is standing dead, exactly as he was when last seen.* BALTHAMOS *is there.*

WILL. Do you think I need anything else?

BALTHAMOS. You need some inner resource to help you recognise my age-old wisdom and respect it.

WILL. What's the matter? You hungry or something?

BALTHAMOS. Angels don't get hungry.

WILL. So you don't want any of this?

BALTHAMOS. What is it?

WILL. Kendal Mint Cake.

BALTHAMOS. I might try a little out of interest.

WILL *gives him some, and* BALTHAMOS *nibbles it fastidiously.*

WILL. Have you and your friend got names?

BALTHAMOS. I am Balthamos, and my friend is Baruch.

WILL. Who sent you?

BALTHAMOS. We sent ourselves. We heard the rumour of Lord Asriel's war, and it inspired us to join him. But we wanted to take him something more, because we're not high-ranking in the heavenly scheme of things. We wanted to bring the knife.

WILL. Have you always been angels?

BALTHAMOS. I was created in my present form. Baruch used to be a man.

WILL. When?

BALTHAMOS. Four thousand years ago. I'm somewhat older.

WILL. So do people become angels when they die?

BALTHAMOS. Mostly not. May I ask the point of this metaphysical speculation?

WILL. My dad's just died, that's the point. What mostly happens when people die?

BALTHAMOS. They go to the world of the dead.

WILL. What's it like?

BALTHAMOS. It's a prison camp. That's all we know. That's all that anyone knows. The Church tells people that, if they're good, they'll go to heaven. But that's a lie.

WILL. He's in a prison camp?

BALTHAMOS. Of course, like the countless millions who died before him. Now that you've loaded up the dead man's property, can we move on? Baruch will be here in a matter of seconds.

WILL. How do you know? Do you read his mind?

BALTHAMOS. I'm *in* his mind, and he is mine.

BARUCH *appears.*

BARUCH. Balthamos!

BALTHAMOS. My heart, my own!

They embrace and sit with their fingers entwined.

Well?

BARUCH. Lyra is in the world she came from, in a cave beneath a range of snowy mountains. I've drawn it for Will.

He gives WILL *a map.*

There's a waterfall where the ice and mist form rainbows. Red silk banners fly in the wind. The woman with the monkey-daemon is keeping her asleep.

WILL. What with?

BARUCH. A potion. Lyra has not been harmed. She's dreaming.

WILL *looks at the map.*

WILL. Good, so I won't need you two.

BALTHAMOS. You'll need us to find Lord Asriel.

WILL. No I won't, because Lyra can read the alethiometer.

BALTHAMOS. Lyra hasn't got the books of reference.

WILL. She doesn't need them.

BALTHAMOS. *No-one* can read it without . . .

WILL. She can. All right?

BALTHAMOS. No, not all right. How do we know you'll go there? You've already delayed it once.

WILL. Do you think I'm just gonna ignore my dad, after what happened? You're not human.

BARUCH. Obviously.

BALTHAMOS. The notion of having a father at all is quite incomprehensible to the average angel.

BARUCH. Let's compromise. I'll fly on, and tell Lord Asriel that you're coming . . .

BALTHAMOS. . . . and I shall remain with Will.

WILL. I don't need *either* of you.

BALTHAMOS. You do. In Lyra's world, you'll need a daemon or you'll look very much out of place. I can be one.

WILL. You mean, change into a bird or something?

BALTHAMOS. That is exactly what I mean. It will be unspeakably humiliating, and I'll do it only when it's absolutely essential.

WILL. All right.

BALTHAMOS *addresses* BARUCH.

BALTHAMOS. The way will be hard. The fortress is surrounded by spirits, by ghouls, by enemy angels. Fight boldly and fly with care. My heart goes with you.

They embrace. BARUCH *flies off.*

Oxford / Oxford. The Botanic Gardens. LYRA *is there.*

LYRA. I was frightened that I'd never wake up, that I'd be stuck in the place that I was dreaming about. There was mist all round me . . . grey mist and a grey sky, and an enormous grey plain, trodden flat by the people there. There were millions of them, young, old, pale, dark . . . all crammed together, all sad and sorrowful.

WILL *is there.*

WILL. 'A prison camp.' The moment the angel said those words, everything changed.

LYRA. Then I saw Roger. He was the only one there with hope in his eyes. He called my name and he ran to me and I tried to throw my arms around him, but they went right through the air.

WILL. I could feel the words I wanted to say to my dad bursting inside me. I had to see him. Had to talk to him. It was my task . . .

LYRA. I said, 'I'll find you, Rodge. I swore it before, and I swear it again.'

WILL. . . . it was my mantle.

Geneva. The Consistorial Court of Discipline. A corridor.
The PRESIDENT *is with* DR SARGENT, *who is nervous and agitated.*

PRESIDENT. 'Quantum entanglement'?

DR SARGENT. Exactly, Father President . . . it's the principle behind the lodestone resonator . . . that the miniature people of Gallivespia use to send their messages? . . . where two substances are identical, if you stimulate one, the other will respond. It will constitute a bomb. No, it will *be* a bomb. We'll take a sample of organic matter from the subject, Lyra . . . a fingernail-cutting, a flake of skin . . . and subject it to a burst of energy . . . . And that will produce a vast explosion in whichever part of Lyra's body the sample came from, wherever she is.

PRESIDENT. Have we got a sample?

DR SARGENT. Not at present. That is the flaw. But once we have captured her . . .

PRESIDENT. Once we've captured her, we'll kill her on the spot.

BROTHER JASPER *appears with the alethiometer.*

Brother Jasper, what are your latest findings from the alethiometer?

BR JASPER. Lyra is asleep in a mountain cave. Her mother is with her. There's a rainbow above them, and a row of red silk flags . . . heathen flags, they're a method of prayer.

PRESIDENT. Which world is she in?

BR JASPER. She's in our world, and so is the boy. But there's half a continent between them.

PRESIDENT. Tell me the moment that you've found their precise location. Dr Sargent, your scientific curiosity has devoured vast quantities of Church funds with very little result.

DR SARGENT *semi-collapses with terror.*

But you will not be punished, at least not yet. You may continue your research. Brother Jasper, pour him a glass of water.

They go. The CHEVALIER TIALYS *and* LADY SALMAKIA *appear. He sends a message.*

LORD ASRIEL'*s fortress. The war room.* AIDES *and* OFFICERS *are studying maps, plotting battle-positions, etc.* LORD ASRIEL *and* LORD ROKE *see the* CHEVALIER TIALYS'*s message as it appears:*

TIALYS. *Your spies present their compliments from Geneva . . . the Church's alethiometer is now dangerously effective thanks to new and skilful reader . . .*

LORD ASRIEL. And?

TIALYS. *. . . . the knife has been taken from Cittàgazze, into the daemon-world . . .*

LORD ASRIEL. To where exactly?

TIALYS. . . . *no further information* . . .

LORD ASRIEL. Lord Roke, are these spies of yours any good?

LORD ROKE. They are Gallivespians of ancient lineage, my lord. I hope you do not equate small size with small ability.

TIALYS. . . . *Lyra is with her mother in a cave in the Northern mountains* . . .

LORD ASRIEL. *Where* in the mountains?

TIALYS. . . . *the Church will send a fleet of zeppelins to eliminate her as soon as the cave has been located* . . . *this will be soon.*

LORD ASRIEL. I don't understand this. Why are they trying to kill my daughter? What's so special about her? What has she done?

STELMARIA. You're jealous of her.

LORD ASRIEL. Nonsense. I'm surprised, that's all. And what's her mother up to? Stuck in a cave! This is a woman who has her hair done three times a week at six in the morning. What does she know? What's she keeping from me?

A new message comes up, but LORD ASRIEL *doesn't watch.*

TIALYS. . . . *a bomb has been proposed for the purpose of destroying distant matter* . . . *the inventor seems unbalanced* . . .

The message goes fuzzy and peters out.

LORD ASRIEL. When Lyra came to me at Svalbard, I was horrified. I'd sent for a child to sacrifice, and the first to arrive was my own daughter. Then the boy walked in the door, and I relaxed. I talked to my daughter and I let her go. Was that a fatal error? Should I have spent more time with her? Should I have brought her here?

STELMARIA. The only thing that matters now is that you rescue her.

LORD ASRIEL. Yes, that's obvious. But where in hell's name is she?

An OFFICER *appears at the door.*

Yes!

OFFICER. Your lordship, an angel has arrived with a message for you. He was attacked by enemy forces on his way here. We think he has news for you.

LORD ASRIEL. Bring him in.

ORDERLIES *carry in* BARUCH. LORD ASRIEL *goes to him.*

I am Lord Asriel. What have you come to tell me? Speak quickly.

BARUCH. My lord, my companion Balthamos and I . . .

He stops.

LORD ASRIEL. Go on!

BARUCH. 'Æsahættr.'

LORD ASRIEL. Yes?

BARUCH. It is the knife . . . the knife you need . . . the Bearer is a boy . . . Jopari the shaman ordered him to bring it to you . . .

LORD ASRIEL. When will he come?

BARUCH. I don't know . . . he disobeyed Jopari's orders . . . he's gone . . .

LORD ASRIEL. Where?

BARUCH. . . . he's gone to the cave where your daughter is held . . .

LORD ASRIEL. Where is it?

BARUCH. Bring me a map . . .

A map is found and opened in front of BARUCH.

LORD ASRIEL. Show me.

OFFICER. It's too late, my lord. He's fading.

LORD ASRIEL. No . . . he's pointing.

BARUCH points to a place in the Atlas.

BARUCH. Oh Balthamos!

He dies. LORD ASRIEL *places a finger on the map.*

LORD ASRIEL. The paper is cold where his finger touched it. The cave is here. Lord Roke, order our spies in Geneva to conceal themselves in one of the Church's aircraft. Captain, order six gyropters to fly to the cave at once. They will capture the knife and bring it here. And bring me the Bearer too. And bring my daughter. Why are you waiting? Go!

LYRA*'s world. Snowy foothills.* WILL *and* BALTHAMOS *are travelling.*

BALTHAMOS. Baruch is dead! Baruch is dead!

He flies into the air.

WILL. Balthamos! Don't leave me! I need you!

But BALTHAMOS *has disappeared.* WILL *gets out the map and studies it. Slowly and stealthily,* BEARS *appear behind him and approach him with hungry eyes.* WILL *turns and sees them.*

What do you want?

The BEARS *confer among themselves.*

1ST BEAR. It's got no daemon.

2ND BEAR. It must be a witch's daemon.

They nuzzle and paw him.

3RD BEAR. Is it spirit or flesh?

BEARS. It's flesh! It's meat! / It's food! Food! Food!

They drool and chomp their lips.

WILL. Get back! I got a knife, all right?

They laugh derisively. IOREK *appears.*

IOREK. What's this?

BEARS. The king!

1ST BEAR. It's a warm-blooded creature, your majesty. We don't know what it is, nor what laws we'd break if we ate it. But we've not eaten for days.

The BEARS *bellow with hunger.*

2ND BEAR. Not a blackbird, nor a fox!

3RD BEAR. We're starving!

1ST BEAR. Kill him for us and divide him up fairly!

BEARS. Kill him! / We're starving! / We want to eat!

WILL. You can't eat me! I'm a human being!

The BEARS *roar in animosity.*

IOREK. That's the worst thing you could have said!

BEARS. We hate humans!

IOREK. It was a human woman who corrupted Svalbard! It was a human man who blew a hole in the sky and let the sun in! So why should you be spared, you shivering sprat, you pale-faced porpoise, you two-legged shrimp?

A chorus of agreement from the BEARS.

WILL. I'll show you. I challenge you to fight me in single combat.

The BEARS *roar with laughter.*

If I lose, you can eat me and no hard feelings. But if I win, you gotta let me go.

IOREK. I will not fight you! It would be shameful! You are as weak as a new-born oyster out of its shell.

WILL. You're right! I am! And you've got all that armour as well! Make it fairer. Give me one piece of your armour, any bit you like. Then we'll be evenly matched.

IOREK. Take this.

He takes off his helmet and hands it to WILL.

WILL. It doesn't look very strong to me.

He draws the knife and slices up the helmet. The BEARS *mutter in fear and draw away.*

I thought so. Total rubbish. I'll just have to fight you without it. You ready?

He holds out the knife in challenge.

IOREK. Your knife is too strong a weapon. Boy, you win.

The BEARS *growl in grudging assent.*

Now show me that knife.

WILL. I'll only show it to a bear I've heard about. He's brave and he's loyal, and his name is Iorek Byrnison.

IOREK. I am Iorek Byrnison.

WILL. I know. Here, hold it carefully.

He hands IOREK *the knife.* IOREK *looks at it.*

IOREK. This is the edge you cut my armour with. It's sharp enough.

He turns it over.

But *this* edge is the most fearful thing I've ever seen. I can't tell what it is, or how it was made. How did you come by it?

WILL. I won it in a fight and I gotta take it to Lord Asriel, to help him win his war. But first, I'm gonna rescue Lyra Silvertongue.

IOREK. Lyra? She's my friend! Why didn't you tell me?

WILL. Because I'm not a sprat or a two-legged shrimp, all right? I need your help, but I won't accept it without a bit of respect. Now look.

He unfolds the map.

Lyra's being held a prisoner in a cave, and it's somewhere up that river and in these mountains.

IOREK. That's where we bears are going. We've lost our hunting-grounds. The ocean is warm, the seals have died, the ice is melting. But I have heard that in those mountains, there are wild creatures a-plenty and snows that last forever. Come with us.

The BEARS *roar in approval.* BALTHAMOS *appears.*

BALTHAMOS. Forgive me, Will. I was disabled by my grief. But one must persevere, even after you've lost the one you love.

The BEARS *roar in awe and back away.*

IOREK. Who is this?

WILL. It's Balthamos. He's an angel. This is Iorek Byrnison, the king of the Svalbard bears.

IOREK. We've heard of angels. We see them as points of light in the Northern skies. But never before have I met one face to face.

BALTHAMOS. Nor I a bear.

They march onwards.

Geneva. The Consistorial Court of Discipline. The PRESIDENT *in full conclave.* BROTHER JASPER *is there with presentation aids at the ready.*

PRESIDENT. Friends in Holiness, and fellow-warriors! Lyra has not been found. The knife has not been found. The only thing that stands between the world we know, and the pit of chaos, is the briefing that Brother Jasper will now provide.

To BROTHER JASPER:

It had better be good.

BR JASPER. I'll do my best.

A map of LYRA's *world appears.*

First, an overview. This is our world. There at Svalbard is the huge connecting route that Lord Asriel blasted through

into Cittàgazze . . . with the environmental consequences
that we've seen . . . drought, storms, melting ice-caps, rising
sea-levels . . . and the opening-up of random windows of no
relevance to this briefing.

A map of Cittàgazze appears.

We're laying the worlds out side by side because it's clearer
this way, though of course they really ought to be occupying
the same space. Lyra followed Lord Asriel through here into
Cittàgazze, while he moved on to the strange, anonymous,
astral world in which he's built his fortress.

A map of our world appears. Other maps follow as needed.

There's a window *here* between Cittàgazze and a curious
world which boasts a parallel Oxford, much like ours. Lord
Boreal used to take this route before the Spectres arrived in
such vast numbers, and so did Will and Lyra in the
comings-and-goings around the knife. *This* is a derelict
Arctic gap, discovered twelve years ago by the shaman
Jopari. Whose importance . . . I'll explain that later. *This* is
the window through which Mrs Coulter carried Lyra back to
our world, and into the cave of rainbows. *That* is the cave!

*He points it out with great precision. There's approval and
applause from all assembled.*

Lord Asriel has sent a force of six gyropters through his
Svalbard window, and they will shortly approach the cave
from *here*. The boy with the knife was taken upriver by the
king of the armoured bears, and they will arrive from *here*.
Our fleet will approach from *this* direction and arrive at
the cave at the same time as everyone else. The battle will
follow. The advantage is to us, because Lord Asriel wants
to *rescue* Lyra, while our aim of course is . . . is simpler.
In brief, dear brothers in faith, your graces, your eminences,
your honour the archimandrite and you, Father President . . .
we stand on the brink of winning two great prizes. Lyra and
the knife. I hope that's clear.

PRESIDENT. Mrs Coulter's actions are suspicious to say the
    least. I want her brought to Geneva for interrogation. As for

Lyra, I want positive proof that she's been killed. I want her head in a sack. Right here. Where I can see it!

BR JASPER. I was about to suggest that.

Near the cave. WILL, IOREK *and* BALTHAMOS *arrive, accompanied by other* BEARS.

IOREK. Listen!

They do.

Zeppelins are approaching from the South.

WILL *listens.*

WILL. Ssh. What's that?

IOREK. Gyropters from the North. We must rescue Lyra now, before they attack.

WILL. Is that the cave?

BALTHAMOS. It is. Baruch was here before us. I can feel his presence.

WILL. Right, this is the plan. I'll go ahead. I'll wait till the cave is empty. Then I'll wake up Lyra . . .

BALTHAMOS. A great mistake!

WILL. I've done it before, all right? I'll cut a window, then I'll bring her back through a different world . . .

BALTHAMOS. Her mother might find you.

WILL. What if she does? She can't do anything.

BALTHAMOS. She can do much.

IOREK. She will enchant you, like she enchanted Iofur Raknison.

WILL. Me? Get enchanted by her? Yeah, that's *really* likely, after she kidnapped Lyra, and slagged her off to her that poncey pal of hers . . . and then she *killed* him! I'm not gonna hang about, you can be sure of that. Just keep an eye out for the monkey.

He walks to the cave. No-one is there. WILL *goes in.* LYRA *is asleep. The approaching aircraft can be heard.*

Lyra? Lyra! Sit up.

She remains asleep. He eases her up.

That's right. Now . . .

He reaches out with the knife to cut a window. MRS COULTER *appears at the mouth of the cave, with her bowl of medicine.*

MRS COULTER. Will! Thank God you're here.

WILL. How did you know my name?

MRS COULTER. Who else could you be? Quick, cut a window. We've got to get out.

WILL. Stay where you are. I'm rescuing *her*, all right? Not you.

MRS COULTER. Why not?

WILL. Because she wouldn't want you anywhere near her.

MRS COULTER. What makes you think you know her better than I do?

WILL. She told me a million times. She hates you. Didn't you know that? Keep away!

MRS COULTER. Oh Will, Will, Will, you're trying so hard to be aggressive, and all I can see is a good, kind, dutiful boy who isn't quite sure who he is.

WILL *holds out the knife, ready to cut a window.*

WILL. Yeah, very clever. I'm taking her now.

MRS COULTER. Take me too.

WILL. No! You've got a nerve even to ask, when it was you that kidnapped Lyra and made her a prisoner.

MRS COULTER. I had to. She's in danger from the Church.

WILL. She knows that! She's escaped them over and over again. She didn't need any help from you. She never asked *you* to turn her into a pet, a zombie!

MRS COULTER. But there's a greater danger now, and she doesn't know anything about it.

WILL. What is it?

MRS COULTER *turns away dismissively.*

MRS COULTER. Oh, cut your window.

WILL *slackens his grip on* LYRA.

WILL. What's the danger? Why's it greater?

MRS COULTER. Thousands of years ago, in a place called the Garden of Eden, a young woman fell . . . in the physical sense . . . and something momentous happened. She and the man were thrown out of that place, and Dust came into the world. Ever since then, the human race has lived in sin. That Fall could happen again. And if it does, Lyra will be the woman.

WILL. Why's that dangerous?

MRS COULTER (*of the knife*). Don't *point* it.

He lowers the knife.

The Church hates Dust. They won't allow that Fall to happen. They'll kill her to make sure it doesn't. They'll kill me too, without so much as a thought. And you as well. You're part of it, Will. You're a very important part.

WILL. What're you talkin' about?

MRS COULTER. Do you really not know?

WILL. No.

MRS COULTER. Then I mustn't put dangerous thoughts into your head. You simply have to trust me.

WILL. Well . . . why're you keeping her asleep?

MRS COULTER. Because, if she woke up, she'd run away, and the Church would find her.

WILL. Why don't you let her decide for herself?

MRS COULTER. It's not as easy as that. I didn't look after her well when she was young. She was taken away from me,

brutally, cruelly. I had to stand aside and watch her being
brought up by strangers.

She moves closer to WILL, LYRA *and the potential
window.* WILL *doesn't stop her.*

You said she hates me. You're right, she does. Even after
all the sacrifices I've made for her. I've had to cut myself
off from the Church, the Church that has comforted and
supported me all my life. But I must protect my daughter.
And if that means keeping her fast asleep, so be it. Wouldn't
your mother do the same for you? Wouldn't she, Will?

WILL. You don't know anything about my mum.

MRS COULTER. I'm sure she looks after you.

WILL is angry and upset.

WILL. I look after her, as it happens. Shut up about her.

Aircraft are directly overhead. Gunfire.

MRS COULTER. They're here. Cut the window. Cut it and let
me through. Now!

*WILL is about to do so, when his entrancement is shattered
by the appearance of half-a-dozen* SOLDIERS *abseiling
down to the mouth of the cave. They are fired at from
outside and one is killed.* WILL *pulls* LYRA *away from*
MRS COULTER *and prepares to cut a window.*

WILL. Stand back! I'm taking Lyra!

MRS COULTER *produces a revolver and aims it at him.*

MRS COULTER. Stay where you are! I'm holding you
captive!

She laughs exultantly. The CHEVALIER TIALYS *and*
LADY SALMAKIA *appear and tiptoe unseen towards her.*

WILL. What, as hostages?

MRS COULTER. Yes, hostages! They all want the knife and
they all want Lyra! You're my only chance!

LADY SALMAKIA *stings her ankle. She screams and falls
to the ground.*

Something's stung me! Oh my God!

LYRA *moves.*

LYRA. What's happening? Where are we?

WILL. You've been asleep. Come on. Get up.

He eases her up.

LYRA. Oh Will, I had such a dream.

WILL. Don't talk. We're getting out. Hold on to me tight. I'll open a window.

He poises the knife.

MRS COULTER. Lyra, don't go!

WILL. Don't talk to her!

He tries to find a snag in the air.

MRS COULTER. My precious, my dear one! Help me!

WILL. Quiet!

LYRA. What's happening?

WILL. Stop her shouting. If I don't concentrate, the knife's gonna break.

MRS COULTER. Lyra! Don't leave me to die!

LYRA. Shut up! He's cutting a window!

MRS COULTER *speaks in* WILL's *mother's gentle, bewildered voice.*

MRS COULTER. Will? Will, what are you doing?

WILL. Mother.

The knife shatters. WILL *picks up the pieces.* MILITIA *of both sides storm the cave.* WILL *and* LYRA *are at the point of being captured when a company of armoured* BEARS *charges in and carries them out.*

End of Act One.

ACT TWO

LORD ASRIEL's *fortress.* LORD ASRIEL, *alone.*

LORD ASRIEL. I dreamt last night of the angel who challenged the Authority all those aeons ago. The angel who failed because the knife that could deliver the death-blow hadn't yet been invented. I was falling with him, falling for ever, into a blackness so intense that it seemed to invade my brain. But I could feel the rush of his wings beside me, and I asked him . . . did he know, had he suspected . . . that from this night on, he would be held responsible for everything bad that ever happened . . . every temptation, every atrocity, every crime? He said he wasn't surprised at all. He knew the system. The recording angels always put the blame on the losing side.

The war room appears. A signal is about to come through from the GALLIVESPIANS. AIDES *and* OFFICERS *listen in great suspense.* LORD ASRIEL *waits, his hand on* STELMARIA.

LORD ROKE. We have a signal.

They watch as:

TIALYS. . . . *the battle for the cave is over . . . your lordship's forces mounted a fierce attack . . . one angel sighted, fleeing in panic . . .*

LORD ASRIEL. Get on with it.

TIALYS. . . . *the Church retreated without the knife . . .*

LORD ASRIEL. And?

SALMAKIA. . . . *Mrs Coulter has been captured by your lordship's forces and is now being brought to the fortress in a gyropter . . .*

LORD ASRIEL. Remind me to put her in chains.

TIALYS. . . . *Lyra and the bearer of the knife escaped capture, aided by a company of giant bears who appeared unexpectedly. The children are safe and under observation . . .*

LORD ASRIEL. Yes?

TIALYS. . . . *I and the Lady Salmakia will convey them to you soonest . . . they will embark within the hour . . . with the knife.*

The room erupts with celebration.

LORD ASRIEL. I've got it!

STELMARIA. *If* they come.

LORD ASRIEL. They'll come. Ever since Svalbard, there's been only one creature that I actually *wanted* on my side who's turned me down. For which I can't forgive her. As for the rest . . . angels arrive in their thousands every day, beautiful, misty beings, their faces radiant with hope. Women and men and six-legged beasts and fantastic monsters that I'd never imagined have pitched their tents on the plain below us. How can Lyra and Will resist? They're only children.

LYRA's *world. Near the cave.* LYRA *and* WILL *are sitting on the ground. They look at the shattered knife.* LYRA *lays out the pieces.*

LYRA. One, two, three . . . seven pieces.

WILL. I know, I did it, remember?

LYRA. How did it happen?

WILL. It was your mum. She made me think of my own mum . . . and my thoughts got split, and the knife came up against something hard. And I forced it, and it flew into pieces.

PANTALAIMON. Iorek can fix it.

WILL. Can he?

LYRA. Sure he can. He can do anything with metal. And he'll
be back in a minute.

They pick up the pieces of the knife. LYRA *looks at them.*

I know you hate my mother for what she did. But in the
cave, I used to drift up out of my sleep . . . and it really felt
like she was caring for me. I must have got some illness,
mustn't I?

WILL. Why?

LYRA. To sleep so long. And there she was, in a horrible,
lonely place, just trying to get me better.

WILL *tells his first lie.*

WILL. Yeah.

LYRA. Don't you believe it?

WILL. I do if you do.

LYRA. Are you telling the truth?

WILL. I always tell the truth.

LYRA. I know, but . . .

The CHEVALIER TIALYS *and* LADY SALMAKIA
appear.

WILL. Look!

LYRA. Wow.

WILL. Are they normal size and far away?

LYRA. No, they're under our noses and they're tiny.

TIALYS. Good morning, Lyra. Good morning, Master Will.

WILL. Who are you?

LYRA. Whose side are you on?

TIALYS. I am the Chevalier Tialys, and this is my spouse, the
Lady Salmakia. We are Gallivespians, and Lord Asriel's
trusted spies.

SALMAKIA. Our question to you is of somewhat greater importance. (*To* TIALYS.) Will you deliver it, my lord?

TIALYS. I yield to you, my lady.

SALMAKIA. Too kind. (*To* WILL.) Have you the knife?

WILL. The knife? Well yes I have. But . . .

LYRA. Oh, that *special* knife? Yeah, 'course he's got it.

TIALYS. Our orders are, to take you and the knife to Lord Asriel's fortress without delay. A gyropter will shortly arrive to collect us.

LYRA. What if we don't wanna go?

TIALYS. Our powers of persuasion are not inconsiderable.

LYRA. Yeah, but he's got the knife, so it's us in charge. If you want to stay and help us, you gotta do as we say. And before we go anywhere, we wanna find a friend of ours, an armoured bear.

TIALYS. We shall bring him to you. But once you've seen him, you must travel directly to Lord Asriel.

LYRA. Oh we'll do that all right.

The GALLIVESPIANS *go.*

You're a rotten liar. It's lucky for you I'm here. It's really important that those gallipot-things don't know it's broken. Then once it's fixed, you can take it to Lord Asriel like it'd never been bust.

WILL. But you'll come too?

LYRA. Oh sure.

WILL. You don't sound very sure.

LYRA. I am! It's just that . . .

WILL. What?

LYRA. Nothing.

WILL. No, go on.

LYRA. Well . . . all that time I was asleep . . . I kept on having a dream. I was in this huge, grey, flat nothing of a place, and Roger was there. He was . . . beckoning to me, calling me, only I couldn't hear him. And . . . he's only *there* because of me . . . and if I could find him, I could help him escape. But I don't know where he is.

WILL. He's in the land of the dead.

LYRA. How do you know?

WILL. An angel told me. He said my dad's gone there too.

LYRA. So what do you think?

WILL. I'm thinking it's a shame. There's something that I want to say to my dad, and I only thought of it when it was too late.

LYRA. It's not too late. We can go together. You for your dad, and me for Roger.

PANTALAIMON. How will you get there?

WILL. The knife'll cut us into it.

LYRA. 'Course it will!

PANTALAIMON. But . . .

IOREK is there.

IOREK. Lyra Silvertongue! You sent for me.

LYRA. Yeah, Will's got something very special to ask you.

WILL. Ssh, ssh, ssh, hang on. Can you see those little whatsits anywhere?

They look round.

LYRA. No, they've gone.

WILL. You sure about that?

LYRA. Quite sure.

IOREK. What is your question?

WILL. I've broken the knife. Can you fix it?

TIALYS *and* SALMAKIA *appear from somewhere unexpected.*

TIALYS. You have deceived us, Master Will!

SALMAKIA. It was dishonourable to lie.

WILL. Well, you never asked permission to interrupt. This bear happens to be a king, and you're just a couple of spies.

LYRA. And if you knew the knife was broken, you'd have probably killed us.

WILL. And we'd never have found the only creature in the world who can actually fix it!

IOREK (*severely to the* GALLIVESPIANS). Well?

TIALYS. Forgive us, your Majesty. The habit of concealment is hard to break. In our world, we live among larger humans who are constantly attempting to exterminate us. Our intentions towards yourself are wholly respectful.

SALMAKIA. We only intend to take these children to Lord Asriel.

TIALYS. And the knife as well.

SALMAKIA. Once it is mended.

IOREK. Let me see it.

WILL *shows him the pieces. He looks at them.*

LYRA. Can you mend it?

IOREK. I *can*. But I don't want to. I don't like this knife. It would be better if it had never been made.

LYRA. Oh Iorek, if you only knew what we wanted to do with it . . .

IOREK. Your intentions may be good. But the knife has its own intentions. In doing what *you* want, you may also do what the knife wants, without your knowing it. Look at this edge. Can you see where it ends?

LYRA / WILL. No.

IOREK. Then how can you know where it will take you?

LYRA. I can ask the alethiometer.

IOREK. Ask it. Then, if you still want me to mend it for you, I will do so.

TIALYS. May I respectfully say, your Majesty, that the knife must be repaired whatever the child decides.

SALMAKIA. But we must not pre-empt the King.

TIALYS. How true, my dear. Let us withdraw to send Lord Asriel our dispatch.

They go.

LYRA. Can they hear us?

WILL. No.

She reads the alethiometer. IOREK watches.

IOREK. What does it say?

LYRA. It's . . . confused. It says the knife could be harmful, but it can also do good. But it's a tiny difference, like the littlest thought could tip it one way or the other.

WILL. What does it say about . . . the plan we made?

LYRA. It says it's dangerous.

WILL. What if we don't go?

LYRA. Just . . . blankness. Emptiness. Nothing.

WILL. How do we get there?

LYRA. It says, 'Follow the knife'.

IOREK. And is that what you want?

LYRA. It is.

IOREK. Then you must help me to mend it.

LORD ASRIEL's *fortress. The war room.* AIDES *and* OFFICERS *pause in their work to watch the latest dispatch from the* CHEVALIER TIALYS. LORD ASRIEL *listens, his hand on* STELMARIA. LORD ROKE *operates the receiving-equipment.*

TIALYS. . . . *The news is bad and good . . . the knife is broken . . .*

LORD ASRIEL. What!

TIALYS. . . . *but repair will be carried out by the armoured bear . . . King Iorek Byrnison . . .*

LORD ASRIEL. Iorek? He can do it. But what was he doing there? How did . . . ?

LORD ROKE. There's more, my lord.

TIALYS. . . . *Lyra and the boy have promised to bring you the knife once it is mended . . . we do not trust them . . . we suspect they plan . . .*

LORD ASRIEL. I don't believe this.

TIALYS. . . . *to travel to some unauthorised location. Transmission over.*

LORD ASRIEL. Lord Roke, instruct your spies to sting the boy to death while he's asleep, and bring me the knife themselves.

LORD ROKE. No, that won't do, my lord. The knife is only effective in the hand of the Bearer.

LORD ASRIEL. Then they must bring him here by force.

LORD ROKE. There's a problem. Once the knife is in working order, he can't be forced to do anything.

LORD ASRIEL. Are you deliberately trying to frustrate me?

LORD ROKE. It's frustrating for me too, my lord. But at least we know the Church didn't get it.

STELMARIA. They don't need it.

LORD ASRIEL. What are you driving at?

STELMARIA. Ask Lord Roke about the long-range bomb that the Church is building.

LORD ASRIEL (*to* LORD ROKE). Well?

LORD ROKE. As I recall, it will eliminate matter at a distance
. . . that's all we learned . . . your Lordship was not greatly
interested.

LORD ASRIEL. But now I am. They failed to kill my daughter
in battle . . . so now they'll try to blow her up . . .

STELMARIA. . . . . and the boy with the knife as well.

LORD ASRIEL. The *knife*!

He rings a bell.

Send in the prisoner. Lord Roke, you will oblige me by
preparing to travel to Geneva. Why, and how, and who you
will be accompanying, will be made clear to you very
shortly.

MRS COULTER *is brought in by* GUARDS. *She and* THE
GOLDEN MONKEY *are tied up and her ankle is still
stinging.*

MRS COULTER. Bound! Half-gagged! Dragged through your
corridors like a convicted felon! You really are a prince of
politeness!

LORD ASRIEL. Free her at once.

They do.

Marisa, I apologise. At times of war, one is apt to . . .

She sees LORD ROKE, *and screams.*

MRS COULTER. Keep it away from me! That *imp!* That *elf!*

LORD ASRIEL. What's going on?

LORD ROKE. My lord, my spies were forced to immobilise
this lady at the start of battle.

MRS COULTER. It was agony! Agony!

LORD ASRIEL. Lord Roke's just leaving, and he wasn't going
to sting you anyway. Calm down.

LORD ROKE *goes.*

MRS COULTER. *Calm down?* Don't you dare patronise me. Where's my daughter? What have you done with her? She was *safe* with me! Who will protect her now?

LORD ASRIEL. We both will.

MRS COULTER. Don't be absurd. You haven't the remotest interest in her.

LORD ASRIEL. She is in danger.

MRS COULTER. I know she is! I tried to tell you that at Svalbard. But you . . .

LORD ASRIEL. This is a new and terrible threat, that you know nothing about.

MRS COULTER. Are you quite sure I don't?

LORD ASRIEL. I am.

MRS COULTER. So it's nothing to do with . . . ?

LORD ASRIEL. What?

MRS COULTER. Her . . . No, go on.

LORD ASRIEL. The Church has developed a long-range bomb. And I'm afraid they'll use it against our daughter.

MRS COULTER. Oh, they will. They have a *very* good reason.

LORD ASRIEL. What?

MRS COULTER. I'll tell you later.

She looks at him beadily.

Where is this bomb?

LORD ASRIEL. It's in Geneva.

MRS COULTER. How does it work?

LORD ASRIEL. I've no idea.

MRS COULTER. Can your spies not tell you?

LORD ASRIEL. I don't have any spies in Geneva. They went to the battlefield. You saw them there.

MRS COULTER. I *experienced* them.

She rubs her ankle.

You could be lying, of course. You probably are. One month ago, I would have known *exactly* what your game was. But something's dulled in me. I've changed. Lyra has changed me.

She fingers the locket around her neck.

LORD ASRIEL. What's that?

MRS COULTER. It's a lock of her hair. I cut it off in London, and I've carried it with me ever since.

LORD ASRIEL. I think that's very touching.

MRS COULTER. You do?

LORD ASRIEL. Oh, yes.

MRS COULTER. So . . . there's a bomb in Geneva, and they're aiming it at our daughter . . . and it's obvious, isn't it, what has to be done about it? You need a spy there. Someone who knows their twisted minds . . . whom they rely on, up to a point . . . so it will have to be me. When shall I go?

LORD ASRIEL. You? No, Marisa, it's impossible.

MRS COULTER. Oh, you're worried about my safety, are you?

LORD ASRIEL. I'm worried about your loyalty to me. You are the Church's faithful servant.

MRS COULTER. Not any more. I hate them. I hate them so intensely that it will be difficult for me to lie to them. But I'll manage it somehow. How do I get there?

LORD ASRIEL. My men will fly you to Geneva as soon as you're ready. They'll collect you the following morning at six a.m.

MRS COULTER. You've worked it all out, I see. One moment.

She looks at her MONKEY-DAEMON, *who is making stabbing gestures in the air.*

What?

He repeats the gesture. To LORD ASRIEL:

Just tell me one thing. What happened to the knife?

LORD ASRIEL. The knife?

MRS COULTER. Yes, after I broke it.

LORD ASRIEL. It will be mended.

MRS COULTER. And you don't want it broken again. Still less wiped out by a long-range bomb. You toad! You schemer! This is nothing to do with Lyra at all. It's the knife!

LORD ASRIEL. I need that knife! I have to protect it!

MRS COULTER. What for? So you can kill the Authority? Ha ha ha. What good will that do? Have you thought about that? No, you don't care. It's all your pride, your glorification, your ambition . . . !

LORD ASRIEL. This is unworthy of you, Marisa.

MRS COULTER. Oh come off it. How would you know what's worthy or not? You tried to exploit my motherly love for your own selfish purposes!

He laughs.

Don't laugh!

LORD ASRIEL. I can't help it!

He laughs.

Your motherly love! You hated Lyra! You abandoned her!

MRS COULTER. I did not! You stole her from me . . . !

LORD ASRIEL. I had to! You were raving mad! You'd have throttled her in her cradle!

MRS COULTER. . . . then you ignored her, you neglected her, year after year, she had no decent company, no education . . .

LORD ASRIEL. You only loved her in that cave because she was fast asleep.

MRS COULTER. What if I did? It's still love.

LORD ASRIEL. No it's not. It's fantasising. So that you won't have to *pretend* to love the tedious little creature that she really is.

MRS COULTER. You don't know what she really is.

LORD ASRIEL. Of course I do. She's . . .

MRS COULTER. Listen to me. There's something new. Lyra is extraordinary. She's unique. If you had any idea . . .

LORD ASRIEL. Oh, she's unique all right. To win you round . . . you of all people . . . the steely-eyed fanatic, the persecutor of children, the inventor of hideous machines to slice them apart . . . to turn you into a fussy red hen, clucking and settling your feathers over her . . . that's quite an achievement.

MRS COULTER. It is.

LORD ASRIEL. And you'll go to Geneva?

MRS COULTER. I will. For her.

She turns to go.

Who won that? You or me?

LORD ASRIEL. We both got what we wanted.

MRS COULTER. So we did. But I'll be back. And then let battle commence.

She goes out. LORD ROKE, *who has been hiding somewhere, appears.*

LORD ROKE. My lord?

LORD ASRIEL. Hide in the aircraft. Don't let her see you. Report to me when you get there.

In the cave. IOREK *is mending the knife.* LYRA *adds branches to the fire,* WILL *adjusts them to focus the heat and* PANTALAIMON *fans the flames.*

IOREK (*to* WILL). Last piece! Hold it still in your mind!

> WILL *concentrates on his mental image of the knife.*

WILL. I've got it! I can see it!

IOREK. Feel the atoms! Feel them joining, strengthening, straightening!

WILL. I feel them!

> IOREK *hammers the last fragments with his home-made hammer.*

IOREK. Now it must cool. Call me when the blade turns back to silver.

> *He places it in the cinders. To* WILL*:*

Come.

> *He and* WILL *walk out of the cave.*

What will you do with the knife?

WILL. I don't know.

> IOREK *knocks him over.*

IOREK. Answer me truthfully.

> WILL *struggles to his feet.*

WILL. We want to go down to the land of the dead . . . for my dad, and Roger as well. But I'm pulled in so many different ways. My mum's ill, and I want to go home and look after her. My dad told me to take the knife to Lord Asriel. And I'm frightened . . . and maybe my fear is pushing me in the wrong direction. Maybe sometimes the frightening thing is the wrong thing, but we don't want to look like a coward, and so we do it *because* it's frightening. I don't know.

IOREK. I too am full of doubt. And that is a human thing. If I am becoming human, something's wrong, something's bad. It may be that I have brought the final destruction on my kingdom. But there is one thing I know for certain. If you want to succeed in the task you have set yourself, you must no longer think about your father and mother. If your mind is divided, the knife will break once more, and I will not be there to mend it.

LYRA *approaches, with the knife.*

LYRA. It's turned to silver.

IOREK. Will has told me where you are going.

LYRA. I've gotta rescue Roger.

IOREK. Your business is not with death. It is with living creatures.

LYRA. Our business is to do what we promised, en't it? I wish I'd never had that dream, and I wish we'd never found out that the knife could take us there. But it can.

IOREK. Can is not the same as must.

LYRA. But if you must, and you can, then you got no excuse.

IOREK. Do as you must.

To WILL:

Take the knife, and plunge it into the stream.

WILL *goes to do so. To* LYRA:

When I first met him, he was too clever for me, too daring. There is no-one else I would be happy to leave you with. If you escape from the land of the dead, you will meet me in the battle at the end of the world. If you cannot escape, you'll never see me again. When I die, my body will lie on the earth, and then be part of it. Go well.

LYRA. Go well, King Iorek Byrnison.

She embraces him and he goes. WILL *comes back with the knife.*

WILL. It's done. It'll work.

She looks at it.

LYRA. It isn't beautiful any more.

WILL. It looks what it is. It's wounded.

LYRA. You ready?

PANTALAIMON. What if you can't get out?

LYRA. If it can cut us in, it'll cut us out again.

PANTALAIMON. What if you gotta die to go there?

WILL. We aren't gonna die. Not with our bodies. 'Cause bodies don't go anywhere. They just stay in the earth and rot.

LYRA. And it can't be our daemons either. They just fade and dissolve.

PANTALAIMON. I don't wanna fade and dissolve!

LYRA. You won't have to, Pan, 'cause there must be a different part. A part that's not our bodies, an' not our daemons. A part that can think about both of them. A third part.

WILL. Our ghost.

LYRA. That's right. Our ghost. We're going as ghosts.

PANTALAIMON. Ghosts are sad! Ghosts are frightening! Don't go!

LYRA. Oh Pan . . . we won't know anything till we try it. You know I love you. I'll look after you for ever an' ever. But we can't be too frightened to do what we've got to.

TIALYS *and* SALMAKIA *appear.*

TIALYS. What are you doing?

WILL. We're gonna follow the knife to the land of the dead.

TIALYS. You may not do that!

SALMAKIA. You must wait for the gyropter.

WILL. It doesn't matter what you think. We're going. You can come if you like, or stay where you are. It's up to you.

He stretches out his hand, holding the knife. Tries a couple of snags.

Not that.

TIALYS. This is forbidden!

WILL. Not that.

SALMAKIA. This is a contravention of the rules for prisoners!

> WILL *finds a snag with an unpleasant feeling about it. The*
> GALLIVESPIANS *continue to protest as:*

WILL. This could be it. (*To* LYRA.) You sure about this?

LYRA. Go on.

> WILL *cuts a window.*

> *A lodestone resonator signal is seen or heard:*

TIALYS. . . . *The Chevalier Tialys regrets to inform . . . Lyra
and boy have escaped with knife to Land of Dead after
overpowering your agents and issuing violent threats . . .
profound apologies . . .*

> *The signal cross-fades with another signal:*

LORD ROKE. *Lord Roke reporting from Geneva . . . vast an-
baric activity taking place in underground laboratory . . .
their weapon complete except for what they call a 'sample'
. . . sample of what is not yet clear . . . will find out
soonest . . .*

Geneva. The Consistorial Court of Discipline. MRS COULTER
*is shown into a cell. She tries the bed, which is hard. She's
about to undress when she sees* LORD ROKE.

MRS COULTER. Lord Roke! Just when would you have done
me the courtesy of telling me you were here? Before I
undressed or after?

LORD ROKE. Before, of course. Do you really suppose I have
some unseemly interest in giantesses? I found the bomb.

MRS COULTER. And?

LORD ROKE. It's based around a cutting device, with a blade
constructed of some unfamiliar metal.

MRS COULTER. That sounds remarkably like Bolvangar.

A knock at the door.

Hide. The President is on his way to interrogate me. I feel quite sick at the thought of breathing the air from his evil lungs.

LORD ROKE *conceals himself.*

Come in.

The PRESIDENT *and* BROTHER JASPER *enter.*

PRESIDENT. Welcome, Mrs Coulter. You must forgive our simple hospitality. Brother Jasper is here to ensure that I do not waste our time by asking you questions which can be more swiftly answered by the alethiometer.

MRS COULTER. I'm sure he's a great improvement on Fra Pavel. In all sorts of ways. Oh, I'm so sorry. Ask me whatever you like.

PRESIDENT. I've been wondering how you escaped from Lord Asriel's fortress with such ease . . . and how you came to Geneva?

MRS COULTER. As I told your guards, I stole a gyropter. I landed it in the countryside not far from here, and the rest of the way I walked.

PRESIDENT. What can you tell me about the mysterious disappearance of Lord Boreal?

MRS COULTER. I'd almost forgotten about him. He and I were in Cittàgazze, and the Spectres killed him. It's what happens there.

PRESIDENT. To what do you attribute your own survival?

MRS COULTER. The power of prayer.

PRESIDENT. Did he tell you anything about Lyra that surprised you? Her secret name, for example?

MRS COULTER*'s hand strays to the locket around her neck.* BROTHER JASPER *watches intently.*

MRS COULTER. I thought that no-one knew that.

PRESIDENT. Yes or no?

MRS COULTER. No, he didn't.

PRESIDENT. What puzzles me most is . . . when you found
your daughter . . . why you hid her in the mountains? It's
true that I was minded to let you keep her . . . but you should
at least have told us where she was. Were you protecting
her? If so, from what?

MRS COULTER *loses control.*

MRS COULTER. From a body of men with a feverish
obsession with sex, that's what.

PRESIDENT. I beg your pardon?

MRS COULTER. You heard what I said. Men whose furtive
imaginations would crawl over my daughter like
cockroaches. Men reeking of ancient sweat!

PRESIDENT. You have one last chance to save yourself. Lord
Asriel plans to kill the Authority. Does that appal you? Does
it fill you with horror and fear?

MRS COULTER. I think, what does it matter? The Authority's
useless. Nobody sees him. Nobody hears him. Nobody cares
what he thinks. The wicked get rich, and the poor and
humble die in their millions without so much as a squeak of
protest. *If* he's alive, he's clearly too old and decrepit to
think or to act or even die. Wouldn't it be the greatest
kindness, to seek him out and give him the gift of death?

PRESIDENT. 'Out of their own mouths they shall condemn
themselves.' Good night.

He and BROTHER JASPER *leave.*

MRS COULTER. Damn! Damn! Damn!

We follow the PRESIDENT *and* BROTHER JASPER *down a
corridor.*

PRESIDENT. The bomb requires the sacrifice of a worthless
human . . . and we've certainly got one. We must redouble
our efforts to find the sample.

BR JASPER. I think we've got it. When she mentioned Lyra, her fingers wandered to the locket around her neck. There's something inside it.

PRESIDENT. Excellent. Wait till she is asleep. Then go to her room. Remove the locket and bring it to me directly.

BR JASPER. But Father President . . . the lady will be in bed.

Outskirts of the land of the dead. The sound of sea-birds.
GHOSTS *are arriving.* LYRA, WILL *and* PANTALAIMON *approach an official,* MR PERKINS. *He has a desk and clipboard.*

PERKINS. Excuse me please! You people are still alive.

He prepares papers for them.

You wouldn't believe the number of living people they're sending us these days. Take these papers through to the holding area . . . make yourselves known . . . and wait.

LYRA. How long for?

PERKINS. Until you die, of course.

WILL. And then what happens?

PERKINS. Then you'll be travelling on by boat.

WILL. Where to?

PERKINS. I'm not permitted to tell you that. Proceed down there, first gate on the left. Move on. Who's next?

They move on.

WILL. Do you reckon this is it?

LYRA. It en't what I saw in my dream. It's more like a transit place.

WILL. Papers! Look at 'em. They're just pages torn out of an exercise book.

LYRA. At least he didn't look dangerous.

PANTALAIMON. *All* of it's dangerous. Let's go back. I wanna go back.

LYRA. Ssh . . . !

They reach the holding area and step in.

Hello?

A family – JEPTHA JONES, *his wife* HANNAH, OLD MOTHER JONES *and some* CHILDREN – *are sitting round a brazier.*

Is this all right? We was told to come in. I'm Lyra and this is Will. And this is my daemon, Pantalaimon.

JEPTHA *looks at them, puzzled.*

JEPTHA. You have not brought your deaths with you.

LYRA. Our *deaths*?

WILL. No, we haven't. (*Quietly to* LYRA.) What's he talkin' about?

LYRA. Dunno.

To JEPTHA:

We're sorry we've come without our deaths, if that's the normal way of things. But we hope you can help us. We're looking for the land of the dead, and we don't know how to get there. So if you can tell us about it, we'll be really grateful.

JEPTHA. Come to the fire. I'm Jeptha Jones. Hannah, I think they're hungry.

They come to the fire. HANNAH *pours soup into mugs for them.*

LYRA. Excuse me for asking, but are you dead?

JEPTHA. Certainly not. Do you think we look it?

HANNAH. We're still alive, like you. We're waiting here until our deaths tell us it's time to go.

LYRA. Where are they?

HANNAH. They're there.

She indicates a little group of ANONYMOUS FIGURES *sitting apart from them.*

They don't bother us much. They keep themselves to themselves.

JEPTHA. Except for our gran's. He's by the fire.

MOTHER JONES'S DEATH *looks up from under a blanket.*

Hello, old pal. Warm enough for you?

MOTHER JONES'S DEATH *nods.*

Before we arrived, we never could see our deaths. We always had them, though, like everyone else.

LYRA. What, all the time?

HANNAH. Oh yes. Your death comes into the world with you the minute you're born, and it stays with you every minute of your days, until it's time to go. It could come at any moment. When you're sick with a fever, or you choke on a piece of dry bread, or you stand at the top of a high building. In the middle of all your pain and hardship, your death comes to you kindly and says . . . 'Easy now, easy, child, you come along o' me.' And then it shows you into a boat, and out you sail.

LYRA. Where to?

HANNAH. Nobody knows.

LYRA. If I want to get on to that boat . . . how can I find it?

HANNAH. You must call up your death.

LYRA. Will I see it? See it in front of me?

HANNAH. It's the only way. *He'll* tell you.

They look at MOTHER JONES'S DEATH. *He chuckles.*

MOTHER JONES'S DEATH. I've heard of people like you, my gal. You don't want to know about your deaths. That's why they stay out of sight. It's their good manners. But they're always there. You turn your head, and they dodge behind you. They can hide in a teacup, or a dewdrop, or in a breath of wind. Not like me and my old Magda.

OLD MOTHER JONES *looks out from underneath her blanket. Her* DEATH *pinches her cheek.*

I never stray far from you these days, do I, sweetie?

LYRA. What do I do, to call up my death?

MOTHER JONES'S DEATH. Just wish.

PANTALAIMON. Don't. Don't!

LYRA. I'm wishing.

They all look round.

JEPTHA. Nothing.

HANNAH. Well, it's probably all for the best. A child like her. Drink your soup.

They drink soup.

JEPTHA. It's strange you got here. How did it happen?

LYRA. Well, my mum and dad were a king and a queen . . . and they were thrown in prison . . .

HANNAH. So you're a princess?

LYRA. . . . and they escaped down a rope. With me in their arms, 'cause I was just a baby. We was attacked by outlaws, and they'd have roasted and eaten me, except I was rescued by Will.

WILL *gets increasingly embarrassed as she continues.*

He'd fallen off the side of a ship, and he was washed up on a desolate shore and suckled by wolves . . . An' then . . .

Her DEATH *appears among them.* PANTALAIMON *hides in fright.*

HANNAH. That's him.

LYRA. Are you my death?

LYRA'S DEATH. Yes, my dear.

LYRA. But you're not gonna take me?

LYRA'S DEATH. Don't you want me to? I thought you wished.

LYRA. I did . . . but I don't want to die, not yet.

LYRA'S DEATH. I can wait. You'll go to the land of the dead in your own good time. And when you do, you'll have your special, devoted friend beside you, who's been with you every moment of your life and knows you better than you do yourself.

LYRA. You don't understand. I want to go there now . . . but I wanna come back.

LYRA'S DEATH. Nobody's ever come back, not for many a year. Why should you be any different?

LYRA. I had someone taken away from me.

WILL. Me too.

LYRA'S DEATH. Everyone wants to see those people who've gone before. And if that is truly what you want, then I can show you the way. But as for returning . . . there I can't help you. You must manage on your own. Do you still want to go?

LYRA. Will?

WILL. Let's do it.

LYRA'S DEATH. Follow me.

He walks on. LYRA, WILL *and* PANTALAIMON *follow on after. They reach the shores of a vast lake.*

This is as far as I can take you.

He goes.

LYRA. Listen.

A rowing boat is heard.

WILL. It's the boat.

PANTALAIMON *howls.*

LYRA. Ssh, Pan.

The boat appears and comes to rest, rowed by a very old
BOATMAN.

Will? You ready?

WILL. I'll go first.

BOATMAN. Not him.

LYRA. Not who?

The BOATMAN *indicates* PANTALAIMON.

I can't leave Pantalaimon behind. I'll die!

BOATMAN. Isn't that what you want?

PANTALAIMON *howls and whimpers.*

WILL. No, that's not fair. Her daemon is part of her. I don't
have to leave part of myself behind.

BOATMAN. You do, young man. The only difference is that
she can see it and talk to it. You will lose something just as
precious, and you'll miss it as much as she does.

LYRA. How will I find him again?

BOATMAN. You never will.

LYRA. What if he waits for us here, and we come back this
way?

BOATMAN. You won't come back this way, nor any other.

LYRA *looks at* WILL.

LYRA. Will?

WILL (*to the* BOATMAN). You're wrong. We will come back.
We'll be the first since nearly ever. So what's the point of
splitting up people and their daemons for the sake of a
stupid rule? Let him come with us, just this once.

BOATMAN. 'Just this once!' If only you knew how often I've
heard those words. How many people do you think I've
taken across this lake? Millions. Millions, millions. There's
not one of 'em does it gladly. They struggle, they cry, they
try to bribe me, they threaten and fight. They say they're not
really dead, that it's all a mistake. They tell me about the
gold and silver they've scraped together, and their powerful
friends, the King of this and the Duke of that. And they all
of them say that, just this once, the rules have got to be
changed. They soon find out there's only one rule that
matters. That they're in my boat, and I'm rowing that boat
to the land of the dead, and I'll be rowing those kings and
dukes as well before they know it. They're just the same as
everyone else that breathes. And so are you.

LYRA *embraces* PANTALAIMON.

LYRA. Pan, I love you. If I have to spend the rest of my life
finding you again, I will. But I can't go back. I can't. I'm
gonna push you away now. I'm sorry.

She pushes PANTALAIMON *away and steps on to the
boat.* WILL *steps into after.* PANTALAIMON *crouches,
forlorn and desolate. The* BOATMAN *pushes off and the
boat moves away from the shore.* WILL *and* LYRA *feel the
pain of separation.*

Oh Pan!

A signal from LORD ROKE:

LORD ROKE. *Brother Jasper removed the locket from
Mrs Coulter's neck while she was asleep . . . His hands
were shaking. This I attribute to his celibate state . . .
The President is in the laboratory with a nervous scientist.
I shall stay on-site and watch.*

*Geneva. A laboratory. There's a large clock in evidence. It's
midnight.* DR SARGENT *is showing the* PRESIDENT *how the
bomb will work.* BROTHER JASPER *watches, looking shaken*

and disturbed. He has the locket. LORD ROKE *is hiding and watching.*

DR SARGENT. This is the separation-device . . . the daemon in this cage, and the human here.

He indicates a large chair with straps and plug-in devices.

The genetic information is sent to the aiming device . . . and it locates the source of the sample.

PRESIDENT. Lyra?

DR SARGENT. She is the target, yes.

PRESIDENT. So she'll be killed?

DR SARGENT. The bomb is still at a primitive stage . . . the effect is crude . . . Lyra will be, not killed exactly . . . she'll be vaporised, along with everything else in sight for up to twenty miles around. The energy which these things produce is quite enormous . . . as Lord Asriel proved at Svalbard . . .

PRESIDENT. That's enough about him. (*To* BROTHER JASPER.) Give me the sample.

BR JASPER. Of course.

PRESIDENT. Are you quite well, Brother Jasper?

BR JASPER. I'm feeling . . . thoughtful, sir. I'm not normally awake so late at night.

He gives the locket to the PRESIDENT, *who opens it and removes a lock of hair, which he shows to* DR SARGENT.

DR SARGENT. A lock of Lyra's hair!

PRESIDENT. Is this enough?

DR SARGENT. Oh yes, one hair on its own would be sufficient. As for the cutting-subject . . . is it true?

PRESIDENT. It will be Mrs Coulter.

DR SARGENT. How very ironic. I must remind you that the bomb can be detonated once only. And once the operation has begun, of course, it cannot be halted. I shall schedule it for six a.m., if that's agreeable.

PRESIDENT. The sooner the better. Brother Jasper, kindly return to Mrs Coulter's room, and replace the empty locket around her neck.

BR JASPER. Father President . . . is there not some more wiser and older and more experienced cleric who could take my place?

PRESIDENT. Do it. And be sure that you get some rest.

The land of the dead. The boat pulls up at a jetty and WILL *and* LYRA *climb out; the* GALLIVESPIANS *hover nearby. Harsh bird-like cries are heard. The* BOATMAN *rows away.*

LYRA. Do you feel it, Will? A big empty space where your daemon was?

WILL. It's worse than empty. It's like a fist punched through my ribs and pulled something out.

There's a door.

LYRA. We can't stay here.

WILL. Better go through.

A harpy – NO-NAME – *perches on the lintel of the door.*

NO-NAME. You are alive! And so-o-o-o sad!

She laughs.

LYRA. What's that?

WILL. It's a harpy. I've seen 'em in books.

NO-NAME. Your mother went mad! And you were so-o-o-o ashamed of her!

WILL. Yeah, well you better be able to fight as well as scream, 'cause we're going through that door!

NO-NAME. Will's mummy is having nightmares! She's all alone! Ha ha ha ha!

LYRA. Let us through!

NO-NAME. You weren't Roger's friend! You thought he was
thick! You just wanted to see your Daddy, and Roger died!

She shrieks with laughter.

LYRA. Who are you? What's your name?

NO-NAME. 'No Name'!

LYRA. What do you want with us, No-Name?

NO-NAME. What can you do for me?

LYRA. We could tell you where we've been. You might be
interested.

NO-NAME (*tempted*). You mean, you'll tell me a story?

LYRA. Yeah.

NO-NAME. Tell me a story I like, and I might let you through.

LYRA. All right.

She starts telling her story lamely:

My mum an' my dad were the Duke and Duchess of
Abingdon, and they was as rich as anything. The king used
to come and hunt tigers in our enormous forest. And . . .

NO-NAME *launches herself at* LYRA.

NO-NAME. Liar! Liar! Lyra liar! Lyra the liar Lyra the liar
Lyra the liar!

WILL *extends the knife and* NO-NAME *swoops away.*

LYRA. What's happening, Will? Why I can't I lie any more?

Other HARPIES *attack.* WILL *drags* LYRA *through the
door and into . . .*

. . . *a vast, grey plain.* HARPIES *cry overhead. The plain is
peopled with* GHOSTS: *standing, sitting, crouching, all grey
and listless.*

LYRA. This is it. It's the place in my dream.

WILL. Are these the ghosts?

LYRA. Yeah. This is everyone in all the worlds who ever died.

WILL. And there's so many kids. It's so sad.

LYRA. Will . . . I just thought of something. When Mr. Scoresby was flying me from Bolvangar, Serafina was talking about me, 'cause she thought I was asleep. There's a prophecy about me. I'm gonna do something special. Something to do with death. A nyal . . . A nyler . . .

WILL. Annihilation. Making something into nothing.

LYRA. That's what I'll do. I'm gonna finish off death for good. Not just Roger, not just your dad. All of these ghosts we're lookin' at, every one. We're gonna cut a window into the world outside, and let 'em go free. So you better make sure that the knife can get us out.

WILL. I'll find some place where they aren't all staring at us.

He turns to go.

LYRA. Will.

WILL. What?

LYRA. I'm glad we're here together.

WILL. Yeah, me too.

He goes. CHILDREN *approach* LYRA.

1ST GHOST-CHILD. You're new here, aren't you?

2ND GHOST-CHILD. Do you miss your daemon?

LYRA. Yeah. But I'm getting him back.

1ST GHOST-CHILD. Everyone thinks that when they've just arrived.

3RD GHOST-CHILD. Don't get any better either.

2ND GHOST-CHILD. We're always thinking about daemons, en't we?

1ST GHOST-CHILD. Yeah, we sit and remember 'em all the time.

2ND GHOST-CHILD. My daemon . . .

3RD GHOST-CHILD. Yeah?

2ND GHOST-CHILD. . . . he used to think he'd settle as a
bird, but I hoped he wouldn't, 'cause I liked stroking his fur.

IST GHOST-CHILD. My daemon and me used to play hide-
and-seek.

Other GHOST CHILDREN *join in:*

GHOST-CHILDREN.

Mine used to curl up in my hand and go to sleep.

I hurt my eye and I couldn't see, and he guided me all the
way home.

Mine never wanted to settle, but I wanted to grow up, and
we used to argue.

My daemon said, 'I'm over and done with', then he went
forever. Just dissolved in the air. Now I ain't got him no
more. I don't know what's going to happen ever again.

There ain't *nothing* going to happen.

You don't know that!

That boy and this girl came, didn't they?

That's the first thing that's happened in years and years!

Nobody knew that *that* was going to happen.

Well maybe it's all going to change now.

Yes! P'raps it'll change.

ROGER *appears.*

ROGER. Lyra!

LYRA. Rodge!

He runs to her.

ROGER. You've come to get me! I knew you would. I been
calling for you ever since I died. The others was making fun
of me every time, but . . .

LYRA. I heard you.

ROGER. How? How did you hear me?

LYRA. I dreamed about you. I tried to hug you, but my arms
went right through your body . . .

She reaches for him. The GHOSTS *sigh, and the* HARPIES
laugh mockingly.

ROGER. Don't try! You can't even touch a person here, it's a
terrible place. There's nothing changes, it's just grey and
hopeless, and them bird-things . . . they come up behind
you, and they whisper all the bad things you ever did. All
the greedy and 'orrible thoughts you ever had, they know
'em all. You can't get away from 'em.

LYRA. Don't worry, Rodge. I'm getting you out of here. Will's
got a knife. It cuts through anything. And . . .

ROGER. Who's Will?

LYRA. My friend.

ROGER. Is he your best friend? Is he better than me?

LYRA. Not better, Rodge. No-one could be better than what
you were. He's just . . . the best friend I can touch . . . or
hug . . .

ROGER. Tell me about it.

LYRA. Won't it make you sad?

ROGER. It might do . . . but at least it'll feel alive.

LYRA. Well . . . Will's the best friend I can get into fights with.
Or share an apple with, or race up a hill, or sit in the sun.

The GHOST-CHILDREN *cluster nearer.*

GHOST-CHILDREN.

Tell us about it!

Tell us about the world!

We've half-forgotten it, Miss!

Tell us!

LYRA *looks round. The* CHILDREN *are gathered around her, listening.*

LYRA. I said 'fight', 'cause Roger and me used to fight the other kids in the Oxford clay-beds.

ROGER *smiles, remembering.*

ROGER. Yeah, we did.

LYRA. There's a row of willow trees along the side of the river, with the leaves all silvery underneath. Even in summer, when it's boiling hot, it's shady down there, and the clay is all sloshy and wet, but dry on top, so you can take a big slab in your hand like this.

ROGER *shows them.*

ROGER. Like that!

LYRA. And there's a million different smells there. Like smoke from where the bricks are burning . . .

ROGER. . . . and the river all warm and mouldy . . .

LYRA. . . . and the baked potatoes that the burners ate . . .

ROGER. Yeah, horrible food they eat . . .

LYRA. . . . and there'd be Roger, me, Simon Parslow . . .

ROGER. That's my cousin . . .

LYRA. . . . Hugh Lovett, the butler's son . . .

ROGER. . . . and Dick Purser, who could spit the furthest.

The CHILDREN *laugh.*

LYRA. Then when the clay was all over us head to foot . . .

She continues. Meanwhile:

Another part of the land of the dead. WILL *extends the knife into the air, looking for a snag. He finds one and tries to cut. There's a hideous, grating noise.* WILL *is terrified. He raises his hand to try again.* JOPARI *appears. He looks well, and is still wearing his shaman's cloak.*

JOPARI. Do that once more, and the knife will break.

WILL. Dad!

JOPARI. Will.

WILL. You look different.

JOPARI. I'm healthy now. Death isn't pleasant, but it has its compensations.

WILL. Aren't you angry with me? I didn't do what you said. I was meant to ignore everything, and . . .

JOPARI. Take me to Lyra.

They walk back.

There's something's happening in the world outside, some kind of threat to you both. I don't know what, but it's big, it's vast. I want to get the two of you out of here.

WILL. How did you know about Lyra?

JOPARI. I was a shaman, Will. And a father too. We know these things.

They see LYRA, *who is finishing her story. Grown-up* GHOSTS *are listening as well as* CHILDREN, *and the* HARPIES *listen on the perimeter.*

LYRA. . . . and washed . . . and scrubbed . . . and put into bed. And we'd none of us had a more beautiful day in all our lives.

ROGER. That's how it was.

The CHILDREN *applaud quietly.*

LYRA. Here, No-Name, you enjoyed that. When I told you a story before, you flew at me.

NO-NAME. You promised to tell me a story. But it was lies that time! It was lies and fantasies!

LYRA. But now you was listening quietly. Why was that?

NO-NAME. Because you spoke the truth.

2ND HARPY. Because it was nourishing.

3RD HARPY. Because it was feeding us. Because we didn't know that there was anything in the world but lies and wickedness.

4TH HARPY. Because it brought us news of the wind and the sun and the rain.

NO-NAME. But now we've read your thoughts. You plan to escape. And there'll be no more stories! Traitor!

The HARPIES *scream and fly at* LYRA, *terrifying the* GHOSTS. WILL *leaps in towards* LYRA, *brandishing the knife, and the* HARPIES *draw back, still squawking and scratching menacingly.*

LYRA. Will! Cut the window!

WILL. I can't! The knife won't work!

The HARPIES *scream in triumph.*

NO-NAME. We'll revenge ourselves! We made this place a wasteland. Now we'll make it hell!

3RD HARPY. We'll hurt you!

1ST HARPY. We'll defile you!

2ND HARPY. We'll send you mad with fear!

NO-NAME. We'll torture you every day until you tell us stories!

The HARPIES *advance on* LYRA *and* WILL.

WILL. Stop! We'll make a bargain. Show Lyra and me and all these ghosts, the way to climb out of this place into the open air. And then forever after . . . you'll have the right to lead every ghost who arrives, all the way through the land of the dead, from the landing-post to the world outside.

NO-NAME. That's no bargain! What do we get in return?

LYRA. I'll tell you. Every one of those ghosts will have a story. They'll have true things to tell you about the things they saw and heard and loved in the life that they've left behind. You can ask them about their lives. And they gotta tell you.

NO-NAME. What if they won't? What if they lie? Can we
    torture them forever?

LYRA. That's fair. Now show us the way!

A GHOST *steps forward.*

1ST GHOST. Not so fast. What will happen to us outside?

Other GHOSTS *join in anxiously:*

2ND GHOST. We'll never survive!

3RD GHOST. We won't exist!

1ST GHOST. We'll be better off down here.

3RD GHOST. Tell us what to expect!

2ND GHOST. We won't go one step until you tell us!

JOPARI *steps forward.*

JOPARI. Listen to me, all of you. We will dissolve, just like
    our daemons did when we died. But they're not *nothing.*
    They've gone into the wind and the trees and the earth and
    all the living things. That's what will happen to us, I swear
    to you. I promise you on my honour. We'll drift apart, but
    we'll be out in the open, part of everything that's alive.
    Well, what do you say?

NO-NAME *spreads her wings.*

NO-NAME. Follow me!

She moves away. Slowly and unconvinced, the GHOSTS *go
after her.* JOPARI *and* LYRA *look at each other as they go.*

A signal comes through from LORD ROKE:

LORD ROKE. . . . *grave emergency . . . Mrs Coulter is about
    to be severed from her monkey-daemon . . . Lyra will be
    destroyed wherever she is by immense explosion . . .
    conveyed by lock of hair . . . one hair is enough . . . repeat,
    one hair enough . . .*

Geneva. The laboratory. The clock shows five to six. MRS COULTER *and* THE GOLDEN MONKEY *are in the respective sections of the bomb: he in the cage, despairingly banging his head against the bars, she strapped to the chair.* DR SARGENT *is adjusting the equipment.* BROTHER JASPER *stands by, assisting. He has a bunch of keys.*

DR SARGENT. I place the sample here . . .

> *He places the lock of hair in a brightly-lit compartment.*

> . . . and now it's time to reveal the daemon-bond.

> BROTHER JASPER *touches a control and the daemon-bond appears, as at Bolvangar.*

MRS COULTER (*to* DR SARGENT). You rat! You snake!

DR SARGENT. . . . pay no attention . . . watch the dial . . .

MRS COULTER. You were nothing when I found you! Nothing!

DR SARGENT. Mrs Coulter, I'm a forgiving man, but I can safely say that seeing you in that chair is the most deeply enjoyable moment of my life in science.

> *Lights flash and the equipment starts to whirr.*

> It's starting. This is it. Quite irreversible. I'll call the President.

> *He hurries out.* BROTHER JASPER *busies himself with something.*

MRS COULTER. Go on!

> BROTHER JASPER *pays no attention.*

> Let me out. What're you waiting for?

> *He ignores her. Sweetly:*

> Jasper? Jasper?

BR JASPER. Don't talk to me.

MRS COULTER. You promised!

BR JASPER. I didn't mean it.

MRS COULTER. Oh yes you did.

BR JASPER. It wasn't me. It was my baser self. Oh, I am
damned! Save me! Save me!

He falls to his knees and starts praying. LORD ROKE
appears.

LORD ROKE. Plan Two, I think.

He stings BROTHER JASPER, *who falls unconscious to the
ground.* LORD ROKE *takes the keys and carries them over
to* MRS COULTER.

MRS COULTER. The hair! The hair! Get it!

MRS COULTER *unlocks herself and releases* THE GOLDEN
MONKEY. LORD ROKE *gets the lock of hair and hides.
The door bursts open, and the* PRESIDENT *and* DR
SARGENT *burst in, followed by* CHURCH GUARDS.

PRESIDENT. What's happening? Get back in the chair!

The GUARDS *menace* MRS COULTER *with their guns.*
DR SARGENT *rushes over to check the sample.*

GUARDS. Back in the chair! Back in the chair.

DR SARGENT. The sample has gone! We must have the
sample!

Bangs and explosions are heard from outside. More
GUARDS *rush in.*

GUARD. Father President, we're being attacked!

The GUARDS *aim at* MRS COULTER *and are about to
fire.*

GUARDS. You knew it! Spy! Witch! Traitor! (*etc.*)

PRESIDENT. Don't shoot her! She's no use to us dead!

DR SARGENT. If we don't find the sample, the whole
operation will blow up in our faces.

PRESIDENT (*to* MRS COULTER). Where's the sample?

MRS COULTER. Why ask me?

LORD ROKE appears with the sample. He stings GUARDS one by one and they fall unconscious. GUARDS point and shout.

GUARDS. It's there! It's there! Look out!

DR SARGENT. Twenty seconds to go!

GUARDS chase LORD ROKE round the room trying to shoot him. At first he nimbly dodges the bullets, but at last he's shot and falls at MRS COULTER's feet. She grabs the sample and dashes for the door. The PRESIDENT, meanwhile, is examining the sample-case on the machine.

DR SARGENT. Ten seconds!

MRS COULTER. You'll never catch me alive!

She runs out. The remaining GUARDS pursue her. Gunfire is heard outside.

DR SARGENT. We must have a cutting-subject! Somebody bring her back!

PRESIDENT. There's no time for that. It will have to be me. Better a world where I am destroyed, as long as Dust is vanquished!

Rapt and exultant, he puts his struggling DAEMON in the cage, then straps himself into the chair. A GUARD rushes in.

GUARD. We're surrounded!

BROTHER JASPER rises to his feet.

BR JASPER. Father President, stop!

DR SARGENT. Five seconds!

BR JASPER. You'll die for nothing! She has the sample.

PRESIDENT. She does not have it all.

He indicates a single hair in the sample-case.

One hair remains.

DR SARGENT. Look out!

*The bomb goes into the final stage. Lights flash, sirens blow,
the blade rises to its highest pitch.* LORD ASRIEL*'s*
RAIDING-FORCE *breaks in, accompanied by* MRS
COULTER.

MRS COULTER. Shoot the machine! Destroy it!

The PRESIDENT *smiles.*

PRESIDENT. Too late!

The ascent from the land of the dead. NO-NAME *flies ahead.*
LYRA, WILL *and* ROGER *follow her lead, at the head of a
winding trail of* GHOSTS. *A menacing rumble is heard. All stop
and flatten themselves against the walls or the ground in fear.*

LYRA. What's that noise?

WILL. Dunno . . . but it's getting nearer.

JOPARI *runs into view.*

JOPARI. Will, take the knife, and find the place where a lock
has been cut from Lyra's hair. Shave it off down to the
scalp.

WILL. What?

LYRA. Do what he says.

*She shows him the place and he shaves it close. The
rumbling increases. The* GHOSTS *cry out in terror:*

GHOSTS. Where have you brought us? / Why did you lie to
us? / We'll be buried? / Run! Run!

WILL. *Now* what?

JOPARI. Cut a hole into another world, any world, put the hair
through it and close up the window. Now!

WILL *does.*

WILL. Fine, I've done that. Maybe you'd like to tell me . . . ?

*The rumble of an immense, distant explosion. Rocks tumble
down.*

LYRA. What was that?

JOPARI. The bomb went off in a different world. You're safe.

WILL. Look.

A vast abyss opens, bathed in golden light as Dust streams into it from above.

What is it?

LYRA. It's like one of your windows, Will . . . but they lead on to somewhere. This is empty.

JOPARI. It reaches down to infinity. The Church has opened up an abyss.

WILL. What's that light?

JOPARI. It's Dust.

NO-NAME. This way! This way!

JOPARI. No-Name is right. Time's running out. Climb on! Climb on!

A chorus of complaints from the GHOSTS:

1ST GHOST. Where are we going?

2ND GHOST. We're lost.

ROGER *has climbed on ahead.*

ROGER. Lyra! Come up this way! There's wind! There's daylight!

There's a ripple of excitement from the GHOSTS, *as they all climb on.*

LORD ASRIEL'*s fortress.* OFFICERS *are looking out from the ramparts in agitation at something approaching.*

1ST OFFICER. It's there!

2ND OFFICER. It's getting closer!

3RD OFFICER. Sound the alarm!

Below, on the battlefield level, LORD ASRIEL *appears.*

LORD ASRIEL. Are our troops on the ground in place?

4TH OFFICER. They are, my lord.

LORD ASRIEL. And the angel-battalions?

5TH OFFICER. They're standing by, my lord. They're waiting only for your signal.

OFFICERS *cross the battlefield from left and right, calling:*

OFFICERS. Stand by for the signal! / Get ready! / Sound the alert!

SERAFINA PEKKALA *appears with a* WITCH *in attendance.* KAISA *flies after them.*

SERAFINA. Where's Lord Asriel? Let me through!

OFFICERS *try to stop her.*

OFFICERS. Not now! / Get back to your place! / Leave him alone.

LORD ASRIEL. What do you want?

SERAFINA. Look what I've found.

Her fellow WITCH *displays* PANTALAIMON, *quiet and motionless.*

It's Lyra's daemon. He's alive. Lyra's alive.

LORD ASRIEL *turns to an* OFFICER.

LORD ASRIEL. Find Mrs Coulter. Give her the news.

The OFFICER *runs off.* OFFICERS *try to drag* SERAFINA *away.*

SERAFINA. Let me speak! There's something you have to do. Everything depends on it.

5TH OFFICER. My lord, we're waiting for the signal.

LORD ASRIEL (*to* SERAFINA). Go on!

SERAFINA. An abyss has opened. Dust is falling into it as never before, and there's only one way to reverse the flow.

Eve must fall. Your daughter must fall. The time is now. The boy is with her. I'll be the tempter, just as I've always known I would be.

LORD ASRIEL. My daughter is *Eve*?

SERAFINA. Listen! You must survive the battle, to find the children and see them safely into another world. Do that, and my sisters won't have died in vain. I must go before the woman arrives. If I see her, I'll surely kill her. Farewell.

She goes. MRS COULTER *runs on.*

MRS COULTER. Asriel, is it true?

LORD ASRIEL. It's true. Lyra's alive.

MRS COULTER. Are you certain of that?

LORD ASRIEL. Nothing is certain. Look over the plain. What do you see?

She looks.

MRS COULTER. There's something new . . .

LORD ASRIEL. It's the Clouded Mountain.

MRS COULTER. It's flying towards us.

LORD ASRIEL. Do you see the mist around it? It's angels, whirling like a vast flock of birds. In a moment, I must give the signal for the counter-attack. And I don't have the knife, and I doubt that I ever shall. But there's something we possess that is just as powerful. It's this.

He touches her.

Our flesh. The angels long to have bodies like ours, so real, so strong, so sensuous. And if we *drive* at them, if we're determined, we can brush them away like smoke.

He turns to the ARMY *around him.*

This is the last rebellion and the best. Never before have angels, and humans, and beings from all the worlds and the power of nature itself, made common cause to build a world where there aren't any kingdoms at all. No kings, no bishops, no priests. We'll be free citizens of the republic of heaven.

The ARMY *applauds and cheers.* LORD ASRIEL *turns to* MRS COULTER.

MRS COULTER. If you'd said all that at Svalbard, I might have come with you.

LORD ASRIEL. So you say.

MRS COULTER. Was it a genuine invitation?

LORD ASRIEL. Yes, of course.

MRS COULTER. Although we hated each other?

LORD ASRIEL. I was never convinced of that.

MRS COULTER. I was. *Completely*. But it never quite stuck. I know there's nobody else I'd rather die with.

LORD ASRIEL. So shall I give the signal?

MRS COULTER. I'll do that.

The mouth of the land of the dead. NO-NAME *looks out into a strange world.* LYRA *and* WILL *look out after her.*

WILL. Just breathe.

LYRA. Amazing.

NO-NAME. Have you no thanks for me?

LYRA. Yeah, I do. You brought us here, and you'll bring the ghosts up here for ever after. And if you en't got a name, that can't be right for a job that's so important. Iorek Byrnison called me 'Lyra Silvertongue' . . . and I'm giving a name to you. I'll call you 'Gracious Wings'.

HARPY. I will see you again, Lyra Silvertongue.

LYRA. And when you do, Gracious Wings, I won't be afraid. Goodbye.

She kisses GRACIOUS WINGS, *who goes back into the land of the dead.* ROGER *appears, with other* GHOSTS.

ROGER. I wanna go first. It'll be all right, won't it?

LYRA. Yeah.

ROGER. I'll be part of the wind and the sun, just like Will's dad was saying?

LYRA. I'm sure of it, Rodge. And when I die, I'll be a part of it with you.

ROGER. That's good. That's *wonderful*, Lyra.

To the GHOSTS *behind him:*

Come on!

He ventures out and dissolves. Other GHOSTS *follow and dissolve.* JOPARI *appears.*

JOPARI. In a moment, Will, you'll go through to the battlefield. But there's something that I must say to you first, and Lyra too. When I left my world, I was as healthy and strong as a man could be. Twelve years later I was dying. Do you understand what that means? We can only survive in the world that we're born in. Lord Asriel's great enterprise will fail in the end for the same reason. We must build the republic of heaven where we are. Because for us, there's no elsewhere.

WILL. I got something to say to you too. You said I was a warrior. You said it was in my nature, and I shouldn't argue. Well, you were wrong. My nature's what it is, and maybe I can't change that. But I can choose what I do. And I will.

JOHN PARRY. Well done, my son. No-one on earth could have done better than this. I'm proud of you.

He comes out and gives WILL *his mantle.* WILL *puts it on.*

Now cut your window.

WILL *cuts a window into . . .*

. . . *the battlefield. Immediate noise and confusion.* FIGHTERS *from both sides advance and retreat. As the battlefield clears,* IOREK *appears, wounded and exhausted.* LYRA *and* WILL *run on.*

LYRA. Iorek!

IOREK. Lyra Silvertongue!

LYRA. You've been wounded.

IOREK. No, it's nothing.

LYRA. Have you seen Lord Asriel?

IOREK. I saw him earlier, fighting hand to hand. But no-one has seen him since the battle ended.

LYRA. Who won?

IOREK. Who can say? The Clouded Mountain has retreated. Lord Asriel's fortress was destroyed. But the fighting is over, and that's what matters.

LYRA. Will you go back to the mountains?

IOREK. No, my child. I was mistaken. My bears can't live in those snows. We must return to my ruined kingdom, and make what lives we can. You children will always be welcome, while my castle stands. Go well.

LYRA. Go well, King Iorek.

IOREK cuffs WILL gently and goes.

He looks so old. And powerless. It's all coming on to us now. There's nobody left. Your dad's gone. Serafina's gone. There's only . . .

WILL. Us.

LYRA. Just us.

They see a crystal casket on the battlefield.

What's that?

WILL. Looks like it fell outta the sky.

He goes and looks into it.

It's weird. There's an incredibly old man inside it. Come and look.

LYRA *goes and looks.*

LYRA. It's an angel.

WILL. Why do you think they locked him up?

LYRA. Maybe to keep him safe.

WILL. Can't leave him in there. I'll cut it open.

He cuts open the casket. They lift out THE AUTHORITY.

LYRA. He's light as a feather.

WILL. Gently.

They put him down. THE AUTHORITY *looks at the knife.*

Why's he looking at the knife?

LYRA. I think he wants you to use it.

WILL. You mean, to kill him?

LYRA. Yeah, to kill him. He wants to die.

WILL. But Lyra . . . there's no need. He's dying already.

They watch.

LYRA. He's smiling.

WILL. Listen.

THE AUTHORITY *gasps throatily. Then silence.*

He's gone.

LYRA. He's free.

MRS COULTER *runs on.*

MRS COULTER. Lyra! We've been looking for you . . . !

She puts her arms around LYRA. LYRA *stiffens.* MRS
COULTER *steps back.*

Well, do as you please. Your father's here.

LORD ASRIEL *appears, in fighting gear.*

WILL. Lord Asriel? I'm Will Parry.

He holds out the knife.

I've brought you this. It's the weapon you need above all others. That's what my dad told me before he died.

LORD ASRIEL. What was *his* name?

WILL. *John* Parry.

LORD ASRIEL. So you're Jopari's son? He started it all. Dust . . . the knife . . . and the Aurora-city . . .

LYRA *raises her hand, like* JOPARI *in the Jordan College photogram.*

LYRA. 'Dust is bathing Jopari in radiance, just as it does to all of us, all our adult lives.' I was there. Hid in a doorway. Sorta like now.

LORD ASRIEL *looks at the casket, and* THE AUTHORITY.

LORD ASRIEL *(to* WILL*)*. You killed the Authority.

WILL. I didn't mean to.

LYRA. We let him out, and he died of his own accord. It's what he wanted.

WILL *holds out the knife towards* LORD ASRIEL.

WILL. Take it, anyway. I'd have brought it before, but we had some problems, and some other things happened . . . and we went to the land of the dead . . .

LORD ASRIEL. Yes, so I heard.

WILL. . . . and we nearly got stuck there, but we climbed and we climbed . . .

LYRA. . . . with the ghosts all grumbling, 'cause they were frightened of what would happen. But they escaped.

LORD ASRIEL. Escaped?

LYRA. Yes, they escaped! We let them out! I did what the prophecy said, all right? The nyalation of death. It's dead, it's finished. And if that en't gonna impress you, then I don't know what bloody will. And I don't care. I'm glad for the ghosts. And I'm proud for myself. And Will.

LORD ASRIEL. You *should* be proud! You've freed the dead! The whole foundation of the Church will crumble. The Kingdom is over!

He embraces her.

Marisa, isn't it something to bring a child like this into the world. And I created her! I inspired her. And Will, let me congratulate you, let me shake your hand.

WILL *is holding the knife; he moves to pass it from one hand to the other.*

I'll take that.

WILL. Yeah, sure.

He moves to give LORD ASRIEL *the knife.*

STELMARIA. Don't.

WILL. What?

STELMARIA. Don't let him have it.

LORD ASRIEL. Give it to me.

WILL *hesitates. With vehemence:*

Give it to me!

LYRA. I think you better.

Pause.

LORD ASRIEL. No, keep it. Stelmaria is right. She's always right. And you'll make much better use of it. Cut a window. Go through it and take my daughter with you.

WILL. You don't understand. My dad told me . . .

LORD ASRIEL. Fathers can be wrong. Ask Lyra if you don't believe me.

LYRA. What will you do now?

LORD ASRIEL. I have a plan. It's just occurred to me.

MRS COULTER *steps forward.*

MRS COULTER. But it's a good one. It's a very good one.
(*To* LYRA.) Goodbye, my dear. Say it's all right between us.
It is, isn't it?

WILL. Lyra knows what happened. She was ill, and you put
her to sleep to make her better.

MRS COULTER turns and looks thoughtfully at WILL.

MRS COULTER. Thank you, Will. That was very nicely put.

She kisses LYRA.

LYRA. Don't cry.

MRS COULTER. I'm not. I'm just . . . You'll be fine.

She touches the locket.

I have this to remember you by. Now go, the two of you.

WILL. Goodbye, Lord Asriel. I'm sorry I . . .

LORD ASRIEL. You did well.

*WILL cuts a window, pulls LYRA through it and closes it
up after them. SERAFINA is there waiting for them, with a
wide bowl of hedge-fruit.*

SERAFINA. Lyra. Will. I've brought you blackberries.

In LORD ASRIEL's *world.* MRS COULTER *and* LORD
ASRIEL, *as before.*

MRS COULTER. You saw the knife . . . and you wanted it
badly . . .

LORD ASRIEL. I did.

MRS COULTER. . . . and then you realised, that if you owned
that incredible power, your republic would never survive. It
would be another kingdom, exactly like the one that you
destroyed, only with you in charge.

LORD ASRIEL. It would.

MRS COULTER. Then you realised . . . that that power, was
what you really wanted. And the only way to save your
soul, was to give it away.

LORD ASRIEL. To Jopari's son and the daughter of Eve. It seemed the obvious thing to do. My entire republic might have come into being for that single purpose.

MRS COULTER. And us? What about us?

LORD ASRIEL. Our part is over. Look.

The abyss appears.

MRS COULTER. Is that the abyss?

LORD ASRIEL. It is.

Golden light streams down.

MRS COULTER. Dust is beautiful.

LORD ASRIEL. It's beautiful and it's doomed.

MRS COULTER. Perhaps they can save it. Perhaps just as Adam and Eve replenished the world with Dust . . . our children will do the same, in whatever Garden of Eden they've found. And if they can't . . . it isn't our world to worry about. It's theirs. As you said, our part is over.

LORD ASRIEL. Aren't you frightened of oblivion?

MRS COULTER. Oh yes. But at least it *is* oblivion. We've got Lyra to thank for that.

They kiss.

Now . . . let's explore.

They leap into the abyss.

An unknown world. LYRA *and* WILL *are sitting on the ground. The bowl of hedge-fruit is between them.* LYRA *and* WILL *each pick a blackberry.* WILL *eats his.* LYRA *looks at hers, then looks at* WILL.

LYRA. It's true what Roger said. You know at once when you like somebody. And I liked you.

WILL. The night on the mountain . . . you were asleep . . .

LYRA. I was lying awake . . .

WILL. . . . and I said to Pan that you were the best friend I'd ever had.

LYRA. . . . and I wanted to say all the same things to you. And then your dad died, because he wouldn't ever be unfaithful to your mother. You'd be like that.

She crushes a blackberry against his mouth.

I love you, Will.

They kiss.

Same world. SERAFINA *looks through her amber spyglass.*

SERAFINA. The moon is high. But the clouds are still. Two children are making love in an unknown world. I look through the amber spyglass and I see a change. The terrible flood of Dust has stopped. It's moving differently . . . there's a current here, a swirl of it there . . . all falling like rain on the poor parched throat of the earth. Life has returned. The world is renewed. The Dust pouring down from the stars has found its living home . . . and those two young children . . . no longer children . . . have made it happen.

Same world. Morning. WILL *and* LYRA *are asleep, their arms around each other.* PANTALAIMON *and* WILL's DAEMON *join them, both as cats.* LYRA *wakes and sees them.*

LYRA. Pan! Oh Pan, you're back!

PANTALAIMON. I thought I'd never, ever find you.

LYRA *embraces him.* WILL *wakes up and sees his* DAEMON.

WILL. Hey, what's this?

WILL'S DAEMON. What do I look like?

WILL. Are you my daemon? Are you? Honest?

WILL'S DAEMON. Pick me up.

WILL *does.*

WILL. Hello.

WILL'S DAEMON. Hello.

WILL. I'll have to give you a name.

SERAFINA *is there.*

SERAFINA. I've done that, Will. Her name is Kirjava. Her shape has settled, I think.

LYRA. And Pan?

PANTALAIMON. I've settled too.

LYRA. You're so beautiful. I can't believe that I got so used to being without you.

SERAFINA. What you did, without knowing it, was what we witches have always done. It's painful for us, but once that's over, we and our daemons can wander free. So can you. You will always be one whole being, even when you are apart.

The DAEMONS *spring from* LYRA's *and* WILL's *arms and crouch sadly at a distance from them.*

LYRA. Then why are they so sad, all of a sudden?

SERAFINA. Because they know what I have to tell you.

LYRA. What?

SERAFINA. The worlds were dying. Dust was flowing away, sucked in by that great abyss in the underworld. Only you could save it. This was your destiny, Lyra. To be true to your secret name. You were tempted and fell, and so the Triumph of Dust began. But it isn't complete. Dust continues to flow away, and all that is good will die unless you stop it.

LYRA. *How* is it flowing?

WILL. I think I know.

SERAFINA. Dust escapes every time a window is cut between the worlds, as though from a wound that goes on bleeding.

WILL. You mean the windows must all be closed?

SERAFINA. That's what I have come to tell you.

LYRA. Not *all* of them, though. Will and me are from different worlds.

WILL. No . . . what we'll do, we'll make one little window, just for us, whenever we need it. And we'll close it as soon as we've used it. That'll be all right, won't it?

SERAFINA. No. Every time you open a window, it makes a Spectre. That's why Cittàgazze was so full of Spectres, because there are so many windows there.

LYRA. We can't make Spectres, Will. There gotta be no more windows.

WILL. Not even one?

SERAFINA. Not one.

LYRA. Then you and me can live in the same world, Will. It'll have to be yours, 'cause you can't leave your mother. But I got nobody now. I'll live with you.

WILL. No! Don't you remember what my dad said? 'We can only survive in the world that we're born in.' That's why he was dying.

LYRA. I don't care. I'll be happy to die, just so long as we're together.

WILL. Do you think I could bear that? To see you getting sicker and sicker, while I got stronger and more grown-up every day? Do you think I could live on after you died? No, never, never.

LYRA. But we can't leave each other, Will! There must be a way! I know! I'll ask the alethiometer. It's bound to know.

She turns the wheels. Stares at it.

It isn't working. What's the matter with it?

SERAFINA. Nothing's the matter. You've lost the child-like grace that made you able to read it. And you'll never be able to read it again in the way you did. But there's a different grace that comes with study. Work hard, work thoughtfully, and the time will come when you read it more deeply than ever. Will, you and Lyra must go into your world now. There'll be an angel there, who you must teach to close the windows. That is the angels' task, to keep Dust safe for ever after. Then you must cut one final window. You and Lyra will say farewell. Then you must break the knife.

The Botanic Gardens in WILL*'s world, just before dawn.* LYRA *and* WILL *are there.*

LYRA. I want to kiss you and lie down with you . . . and sleep . . . and wake up with you every day of my life until I die.

WILL. I'll always love you. And when I die, I'll drift about for ever, all my atoms, till they mix with yours.

LYRA. Every atom of you, every atom of me.

Pause.

WILL. It's time.

LYRA. Come on, Pan.

She picks up PANTALAIMON.

If we meet someone that we like, later on, we gotta be good to them, and not make comparisons. But . . . once a year . . . just once a year . . . we could both come here, to the Botanic Gardens, on Midsummer night at midnight, . . . and talk till dawn, just like now, as though we were together again. Because we *will* be.

WILL. I will. I promise. Wherever I am in the world, I'll come back here.

LYRA. At midnight.

WILL. Till the following dawn.

LYRA. For as long as I live.

WILL. For as long as I live.

He cuts a window.

LYRA. Goodbye.

WILL. Goodbye.

> LYRA *goes through. They stand looking at each other.*
> BALTHAMOS *is there.*

BALTHAMOS. Now you must close it.

LYRA. Close it.

> WILL *closes the window.* LYRA *turns away in tears.*

BALTHAMOS. It will be the work of my lifetime to close
them all. But one must persevere, even after you have lost
the one you love. Now you must break the knife.

> WILL *extends the knife into the air.*

WILL. How?

BALTHAMOS. Do as you did before. Think of whatever is
most important to you. Then try to cut.

WILL. Lyra.

> *The knife shatters. Dawn breaks. We're in the present day.*

I wanted to go through after you.

LYRA. I wanted to stay.

WILL. But then I remembered what my dad said. There's no
elsewhere . . .

LYRA. You must be where you are . . .

WILL. . . . and where you are is the place that matters most of
all . . .

LYRA. 'Cause it's the only place where you can make . . .

WILL. . . . where you can build . . .

LYRA. . . . where you can share . . .

BOTH. . . . the republic of heaven.

> *Two clocks are heard striking.* LYRA *picks up*
> PANTALAIMON. *She and* WILL *pass each other and walk*
> *out of sight.*

> *End of Play.*

Afterword

This published version of the play is pretty well exactly the same as the version played at the National Theatre. If there are any differences, they are due to changes made late in rehearsal. The introduction I planned to provide turned out to be very difficult to write. I puzzled for quite some time before I realised why this was. It was because the pleasures and difficulties of adaptation, which were what I was going to write about, were shared with too many other people for me to claim them as my own. So here instead is a short factual account of how it all came about.

About two years ago, Nicholas Hytner asked me whether I had read *His Dark Materials*. I told him I had, and I went on to say that the audacity of the books, and their immediacy, and the apparent impossibility of putting them on stage at all meant that they simply had to be done at the National. I had no idea that Nick was already planning to do just that. I wouldn't have been so eloquent if I'd known. It was only later, when he rang me to say that the rights had now been cleared, and to ask if I'd be interested in writing the stage version, that I realised that I'd been pitching for the job without knowing it.

I said 'yes' at once, for three reasons. The first was the books. The second was that there was nothing hypothetical about Nick's offer: the dates were fixed and the show would happen. Thirdly, I knew that it would be the exact opposite of writing a play of my own. It would be like writing the screenplay for a huge movie or the libretto for a big-budget musical. I'd be in the workshop, or on the rehearsal-room floor, being pushed and challenged and being forced to collaborate. This felt very attractive.

I started writing in July 2002, and the first workshop was held over three weeks that November. Three more workshops followed over the next ten months. Some of the questions they addressed were to do with overall presentation. How to do the

daemons? Where to divide the action between the plays? Choric
narrative, or just stick to dialogue? But every new draft that
I brought in was stood up for inspection, stripped, examined
in detail and re-clothed. Giles Cadle the set designer, Michael
Curry the puppet-creator, Aletta Collins the choreographer and
associate director, Jonathan Dove the composer, Jon Morrell
the costume designer and Paule Constable the lighting designer
all had their effect on the script. Every workshop was fuelled
by Nick Hytner's optimism, his ferocious analysis, and his
grasp of the grand arc of the story and the emotional realities
that form it. His influence on the shape of the plays is great,
and there are now many things about them which neither he
nor I can claim any credit for, since neither of us remembers
which of us first thought of them.

Nick Drake read the script in several drafts and gave good advice.
Andrew Steggall helped me at an early stage by compiling a
vast concordance of phrases, descriptions and references from
the books. He also came up with some radical thoughts about
the structure of the show, of which at least one has endured
through many rewrites and now appears in it.

Philip Pullman has been supportive and encouraging from the
moment the project started. It must be strange to see your
writing changing shape to fit a medium as different as the play
is from the novel. But Philip's occasional words of advice have
never reflected this, and have always led us closer towards
creating a piece of theatre that stands up in its own right, not
as a tame shadow of the novels.

Nicholas Wright